THE RISE OF NATIONS IN THE SOVIET UNION

THE RISE OF NATIONS
IN THE SOVIET UNION

American Foreign Policy & the Disintegration of the USSR

EDITED BY
MICHAEL MANDELBAUM

COUNCIL ON FOREIGN RELATIONS PRESS

NEW YORK

COUNCIL ON FOREIGN RELATIONS BOOKS

The Council on Foreign Relations, Inc., is a nonprofit and nonpartisan organization devoted to promoting improved understanding of international affairs through the free exchange of ideas. The Council does not take any position on questions of foreign policy and has no affiliation with, and receives no funding from, the United States government.

From time to time, books and monographs written by members of the Council's research staff or visiting fellows, or commissioned by the Council, or written by an independent author with critical review contributed by a Council study or working group are published with the designation "Council on Foreign Relations Book." Any book or monograph bearing that designation is, in the judgment of the Committee on Studies of the Council's Board of Directors, a responsible treatment of a significant international topic worthy of presentation to the public. All statements of fact and expressions of opinion contained in Council books are, however, the sole responsibility of the author.

If you would like more information about Council publications, please write the Council on Foreign Relations, 58 East 68th Street, New York, NY 10021, or call the Publications Office at (212) 734-0400.

Library of Congress Cataloguing-in-Publication Data

The Rise of nations in the Soviet Union : American foreign policy and
   the disintegration of the USSR / edited by Michael Mandelbaum.
      p. cm.
   Includes index.
   ISBN 0-87609-100-1 : $14.95
      1. United States—Foreign relations—Soviet Union.   2. Soviet
Union—Foreign relations—United States.   3. Nationalism—Soviet
Union.   4. Soviet Union—Politics and government—1985–
I. Mandelbaum, Michael.   II. Council on Foreign Relations.
E183.8.S65R57 1991
327.73047'09'049—dc20   91–418
                                                                                CIP

92   93   94   95   96   PB   10   9   8   7   6   5   4   3   2

Cover Design: Whit Vye

CONTENTS

NORTH SEA

NORWAY

GERMANY

SWEDEN

CZECHOSLOVAKIA

BALTIC SEA

FINLAND

POLAND

BARENTS SEA

HUNGARY

•Riga
•Tallinn
•Vilnius
ESTONIA
•Leningrad
LITHUANIA
•Minsk
LATVIA
BELORUSSIA

NOVAYA ZEMLYA

ZEMLYA FRANTSA IOSIFA

KAR

ROMANIA

MOLDOVA
•Kishinev
•Kiev
•Odessa
UKRAINE

•Moscow

•Gorky

URAL MOUNTAINS

OB

BLACK SEA

VOLGA

•Sverdlovsk

TURKEY

GEORGIA
•Tbilisi

TOBAL

RUSSIAN

ARMENIA
Yerevan

IRAQ

AZERBAIJAN
•Baku

CASPIAN SEA

URAL SEA

KAZAKHSTAN

IRTYSH

•Novosibirsk

TURKMENISTAN

UZBEKISTAN

•Ashkhabad

IRAN

Tashkent•
•Frunze
•Alma Ata

CHINA

•Dushanbe
TAJIKISTAN
KIRGHIZIA

AFGHANISTAN

PAKISTAN

ARABIAN SEA

INDIA

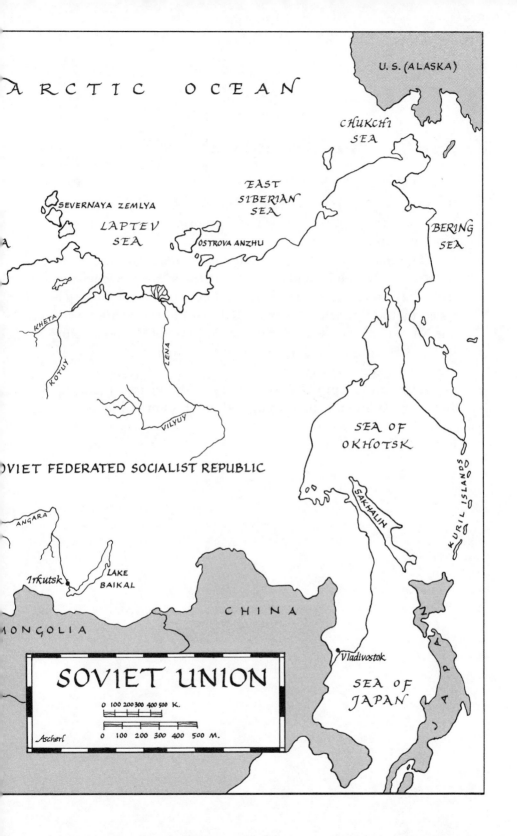

ARCTIC OCEAN

U.S. (ALASKA)

CHUKCHI SEA

EAST SIBERIAN SEA

BERING SEA

SEVERNAYA ZEMLYA

LAPTEV SEA

OSTROVA ANZHU

A

KHETA

KOTUY

LENA

VILYUY

SEA OF OKHOTSK

OVIET FEDERATED SOCIALIST REPUBLIC

ANGARA

KURIL ISLANDS

SAKHALIN

Irkutsk

LAKE BAIKAL

CHINA

MONGOLIA

Vladivostok

J A P A N

SEA OF JAPAN

SOVIET UNION

0 100 200 300 400 500 K.

0   100   200   300   400   500 M.

Ascherl

ACKNOWLEDGEMENTS

This volume is part of the Council on Foreign Relations Project on East-West Relations, which is supported by the Carnegie Corporation.

The chapters were first presented as papers at a symposium on Soviet Nationalities and American Foreign Policy held in New York City on October 25–26, 1990. The symposium was organized by the Council on Foreign Relations in cooperation with the Nationality and Siberian Studies Program of Columbia University's Harriman Institute. A list of participants in the symposium is in Appendix II.

The editor is grateful to Theresa F. Weber for organizing the symposium and supervising the publication of the book.

1

INTRODUCTION

Michael Mandelbaum

During the Cold War, American relations with the Soviet Union were as Karl von Clausewitz characterized the art of fighting a shooting war: simple but difficult. The Western approach to Soviet foreign policy was opposition to all that Moscow sought to do beyond its borders, tempered with caution induced by the power of nuclear weapons.

The American and Western attitude toward Soviet internal affairs was one of complete disapproval. The political system that Lenin had founded, Stalin had built, and Khrushchev and Brezhnev had partly redesigned had no redeeming features whatsoever in Western eyes. Nevertheless, the West, for all its distaste for that system, made little effort to change it beyond protesting the mistreatment of the few brave souls who dared to challenge it directly.

Then, in 1985, Mikhail Gorbachev came to power and turned Soviet-American relations upside down. His "new thinking" about military affairs led to arms negotiations in which the Soviet side conceded that it was overarmed and agreed in principle to the sharp and one-sided reductions that for decades the West had claimed were needed for a stable balance of military power.

He reversed his country's policies of the 1970s and 1980s in the Third World by using Soviet influence to move conflicts in southern Africa, Southeast Asia, and Central America toward resolution and by withdrawing his army from Afghanistan.

Of greatest importance, he did not seek to block the overthrow of Soviet-sponsored communist regimes in Eastern Europe or their replacement with freely elected governments. The end of communist control there in 1989 removed the original and most significant cause of the Cold War.

At home, his policies of fostering wider political discussion, holding elections that were relatively free by historic Soviet standards, and permitting virtually uninhibited emigration eased the most objectionable features of the Soviet political system and seemed to place the country on the path to democracy.

But this happy procession of reform ran aground on an intractable issue that not only caused Gorbachev to change his course and inflamed passions throughout the country, but also created grievous political tensions and ultimately violence. The disorder mounted steadily until, by 1991, the Soviet Union seemed headed toward civil war. This explosive issue was the multinational character of the Soviet state.

THE RISE OF SOVIET NATIONS

Isolated expressions of non-Russian dissatisfaction with one or another of Moscow's policies had become, by the first part of 1991, a serious challenge to the very existence of the Soviet Union.

The first episode occurred in December 1986, in Kazakhstan, where Gorbachev's decision to replace an ethnic Kazakh with a Russian as Communist Party leader provoked demonstrations in the capital, Alma-Ata. The next year, 700 Crimean Tatars, a people Stalin evicted from their homeland during World War II, staged a rally in Red Square to publicize their desire to return.

The first outbreak of violence on a large scale took place in the Caucasus. In 1988, hundreds of thousands of Armenians gathered in Yerevan and other cities in the republic to demand that Nagorno-Karabakh, a largely Armenian enclave in the neighboring republic of Azerbaijan, be transferred to the jurisdiction of Armenia. Rallies in opposition to this demand took place in Azerbaijan, and the protests led to violence between the two communities. By 1990, tens of thousands of Armenians had been forced to flee Azerbaijan, and comparable numbers of Azerbaijanis had become refugees from Armenia.

In the Baltic republics, national self-assertion was directed at Russians and at the Soviet Union. By 1989, nationalist sentiment there was so strong that 2 million people formed a human chain across Lithuania, Latvia, and Estonia to mark the 50th anniversary of the Nazi-Soviet pact that had consigned them to involuntary membership in the Soviet Union.

By the end of that year, national fronts—political organizations that were the functional equivalents of political parties—had emerged in several of the non-Russian republics. The Union-wide elections to the republican supreme soviets the following year brought many of their members to power. By the end of 1990, all fifteen Soviet republics—including the huge Russian Soviet Federated Socialist Republic (RSFSR), under the leadership of Boris Yeltsin—had proclaimed their sovereignty; the purpose of these proclamations was to claim far more power for the republican governments than Moscow had ever granted them.

The Baltic republics and the republic of Georgia went even further. They announced their intention to secede entirely from the Soviet Union. While proposing a new treaty among the constituent republics that would give more authority to the republican governments, Gorbachev insisted that he would not allow the country to break up. At the beginning of 1991, he authorized the dispatch to Lithuania and Latvia of paramilitary forces, which killed more than a dozen people there. The West protested the killings. Thus, six years after he had come to power, the national question had become the Soviet leader's principal preoccupation and the focus of sharp disagreement with the country with which Gorbachev had ended the Soviet Union's bitter 40-year conflict—the achievement for which he had received the Nobel Peace Prize the previous year.

The rise of the national question was an ironic development in East-West relations. The multinational character of the Soviet state and the political aspirations of the non-Russians had not concerned Mikhail Gorbachev when he came to power. An ethnic Russian who had never lived outside the RSFSR, he had no appreciation of the force of nationalist sentiment beyond Russia's borders and turned out to be inept at responding to it.

Nor had this issue been a contentious one in Soviet-American relations. From time to time, the West had taken note of it. In the nineteenth century, the Russian empire was widely known in Europe as the prison house of nations, and President Ronald Reagan called the Soviet Union an "evil empire." Mr. Reagan's political emphasis, however, was on the adjective rather than the noun, and throughout the Cold War, the national rights of the non-Russians—even the Balts, whose incorporation into the Soviet Union the United States had always deemed illegitimate— had never been an important item on the East-West diplomatic agenda.

To compound the irony of the rise of nations in the Soviet Union, the multinational character of the Soviet state did not originate in the 1917 revolution and was not even a distinctly communist contribution to Russian history. It was a centuries-old legacy of the tsars, although one that the Bolsheviks had fought to retain. Thus Mikhail Gorbachev, who had been bold and resolute in undoing the work of Brezhnev, of Stalin, and even, up to a point, of Lenin, finally balked when it came to discarding the achievements of Peter I and Catherine the Great.

The subject of this book is the fate of that imperial legacy in the Soviet Union of today and its effect on the West, particularly the United States. Each chapter offers an analysis of the national question, a discussion of the course it is likely to follow, and some thoughts on how the West and the United States should respond as it unfolds.

The essays approach the subject from different perspectives. The first, by Sergei Maksudov & William Taubman, provides a historical overview of the multinational character of Russia and the Soviet Union, with special attention to the similarities and differences between the present moment and the historical period it most closely resembles—the years immediately following the revolution of 1917.

Next come two essays that assess the strength of nationalism in different parts of this huge country. Alexander Motyl writes about the "Soviet West"—the Baltics, the Slavic republics (Belorussia, the Ukraine, and Russia), and Moldova (formerly Moldavia). Ronald Suny surveys the "Soviet South"— Armenia, Azerbaijan, and Georgia (all in Transcaucasia) and the five largely Muslim republics of Central Asia (Kazakhstan, where Russians outnumber Kazakhs, Uzbekistan, Tajikistan, Turkmenistan, and Kirghizia). Finally, Jeremy Azrael addresses directly the dilemmas and choices that the national question poses for the foreign policy of the United States.

ROOTS OF NATIONALISM

Although it caught the West and the Soviet leadership off guard, the rise of nations in the Soviet Union should not have come as a surprise, for the Soviet state is the last of a political species that once dominated the world but is now virtually extinct: the multi-national empire. The question that the surge of nationalist activity there properly poses is not why it is happening at all, but why it did not happen until now.

The beginning of the answer is that Gorbachev's policies have severely damaged the major props of the communist regime. The Soviet Union has rested, as Maksudov & Taubman note, largely on the "pillars" of ideology and dictatorship. The first has fallen victim to glasnost and democratization; orthodox Marxism-Leninism is almost entirely discredited. The second has been dramatically reduced.

At the same time, nationalism itself has become an increasingly potent force throughout the Soviet Union. This has occurred partly by default, Motyl argues: the ruling ideology has collapsed, and no other focus of political allegiance is available. Nationalism grew in strength throughout the Soviet period, however, even when orthodoxy still reigned. As Suny notes, by creating administrative units along national lines, giving national languages official status, and recruiting local political elites from the indigenous populations, the Soviet authorities unwittingly helped to establish the infrastructure of nationalism. If imperial Russia was the prison house of nations, its Soviet successor has also been, and entirely unintentionally, the nursery of nationalism.

The country's economic collapse has also fortified the drive for autonomy and independence among the constituent republics of the Soviet Union. Economic logic would seem to point in the opposite direction. Republics should, in theory, have an interest in preserving some kind of association to take advantage of a large integrated market. That is the clear trend, after all, in Western Europe.

Soviet economic deterioration had become so marked by 1990, however, that many had come to see membership in the Union as an intolerable burden all apart from any desire for national autonomy. Only by escaping from the tyranny of central planning and the sway of the worthless ruble, more and more people concluded, could they hope to achieve prosperity for themselves. The republics had become, in a sense, economic refugees from the Soviet Union.

IMPERIAL DISINTEGRATION

The crumbling of Marxism-Leninism, the unclenching of the iron fist that had enforced rigid communist rule for 70 years, and the ongoing economic collapse are the functional equivalents for the Soviet Union of the two world wars of this century, which compelled the other great multinational empires to disband because they were either defeated or severely weakened. How those other empires ended provides some clues to the likely course of events in the Soviet Union. They are not particularly happy precedents.

The American, British, and French empires ended more or less peacefully, although that judgment needs considerable qualification in the case of France, which fought and lost a bitter war with the Vietnamese communists in the first half of the 1950s and went to the brink of civil conflict over the bloody effort from 1958 to 1962 to keep control of Algeria.

For the Soviet Union, the process of decolonization is likely to prove more difficult than it was for any of these three. As the descendant of the tsarist imperial domains, the Soviet empire is a much older one than those over which the United States, Britain, and France presided. The Western empires began as nation-states that, during the nineteenth century, came to govern foreign territories. Russians ruled over non-Slavs from the sixteenth century and never in their history had a strictly national, nonimperial identity. Moreover, the American, British, and French empires were geographically separated from the home country. The Soviet empire is geographically contiguous. No buffer of water separates Russia from the Ukraine, Kazakhstan, and the other provinces, making the task of disengaging from them all the more difficult.

As an old, land-based state whose rulers historically defined their role in imperial, rather than merely national, terms, the Soviet Union of today more closely resembles the vanished empires of the Austrian Hapsburgs and the Ottoman Turks. Their examples are also not promising for the prospects for the peaceful evolution of the territories that Moscow governs. Although they perished in World War I, the Hapsburg and Ottoman states left in their wake political conflicts that persist to the present day. In 1991, there was instability in the former Hapsburg domains in eastern and southern Europe, in part because of the decline of the Soviet power that had helped to enforce order there for decades. Similarly, the treacherous, violent politics of the Arab world that produced the war in the Persian Gulf had their roots in the centuries-long Ottoman rule in the Middle East.

Although they left persistent political conflicts in their wake, these empires disappeared both abruptly and completely; their rulers suffered decisive military defeats. The Russian masters of the Soviet Union are unlikely to be defeated in the same way. Other countries will not be able to dictate the fate of the Soviet Union as the victorious allies did—or tried to do—after World War I in the case of the Hapsburg and Ottoman empires. The 1920 treaties of Trianon and Sèvres at least offered blueprints— flawed though they were—for the disposition of the Austrian and Turkish imperial territories, respectively.

Yet another feature of the national question portends trouble. The USSR contains large diasporas: an estimated 60 million people live outside their home republics, of whom approximately 25 million are Russians. Historically, when imperial authority has collapsed, large movements of populations have occurred, as minorities have left newly independent states—or been forced out by the numerically dominant groups. This has already happened in the Caucasus, where most Armenians have left Azerbaijan and most Azerbaijanis have fled Armenia. Because the number of nonnationals scattered throughout the republics is so large, the potential exists for disaster: millions of refugees and communal violence on a scale not seen since the partition of India in 1947.

NATIONAL DIVERSITY

While in India three major communities were involved in the upheaval—Hindus, Muslims, and Sikhs—the Soviet Union is more diverse. It consists not only of fifteen separate republics, each with its own language, but also of more than 100 distinct and officially recognized groups. The republics differ in size, geography, religion, and history. They also differ widely in the social and political changes that have taken place in the Gorbachev era, and especially in the strength of local sentiment in favor of independence.

The most Western, the most democratic, and the most deeply committed to independence are the Baltic republics. Their claims to separate statehood are strongest in American eyes. They are also tiny, together comprising only slightly more than 2 percent of the Soviet population.

The largest republics are the Slavic ones. Some 54 million people live in the Ukraine, and much of Soviet industry and agriculture is located there. The secession of the Ukraine, unlike Baltic independence, would deal a mortal blow to the Soviet Union as it now exists. Some Ukrainians, many associated with the nationalist movement Rukh, favor secession. Rukh is strongest in the western districts of the republic, which were part of Poland before the war; in these areas, the Ukrainian language predominates and most people belong to the Uniate church, a branch of Catholicism. These districts comprise, however, only about 15 percent of the Ukrainian population. The eastern and, to a lesser extent, central parts of the republic are more Russified.

The most important republic for the future of the Soviet Union is the RSFSR, which, with half the country's population and two-thirds of its territory, has dominated the Soviet Union, as it earlier dominated the Russian empire. Russian nationalism is a growing force in Soviet affairs. It has taken several forms, which display a range of attitudes toward the idea of maintaining the Union as a multinational state. Among these is a historically unprecedented strain of nonimperial nationalism, which is willing to contemplate a future without the non-Russian, or at least the non-Slavic, provinces that the tsars subdued and governed over the centuries. This is the position of Boris Yeltsin.

To the south, the Armenians and Georgians of the Caucasus are similar to the Baltic peoples in that they are Christian and oriented to the West. The Georgians seek full independence. While relations among the three Baltic peoples have been cordial and cooperative, the Caucasus has been the scene of considerable violence, particularly between Armenians and Azerbaijanis.

The upheavals of the Gorbachev era have had the least impact in the five Islamic republics of Central Asia: Kazakhstan, Uzbekistan, Turkmenistan, Tajikistan, and Kirghizia. To be sure, the years since 1985 have not left these republics entirely untouched. Uzbeks have founded a nationalist movement called Birlik. Conflict has arisen between and among the groups of Central Asia—for example, between Uzbeks and Tajiks. In contrast to the situation in much of the rest of the country, however, traditional communists still hold local power there. For the most part, moreover, the loyalties of the peoples of this region seem to be cultural and religious rather than national. They see themselves more as Muslims than as Uzbeks, or Turks, or (as in the case of the Tajiks) Persian speakers.

IMPLICATIONS FOR WESTERN POLICY

The unexpected and unpredictable rise of nations in the Soviet Union presents Western policymakers with three sets of issues.

First, the question of Baltic independence, which moved to the center of Soviet-American concerns at the beginning of 1991, was similar to problems that the United States and the West faced in dealing with the Soviet Union during the Cold War. The West was bound to endorse the Baltic peoples' right to independence. But Washington's support for the Balts risked alienating Moscow, thus ending the close cooperation on international issues the two governments had achieved during the Gorbachev era.

During the Cold War, American administrations had to balance the moral and political imperative of speaking out and acting in response to Soviet violations of the rights of its own citizens against the need to conclude international agreements to stabilize the rivalry between the two great nuclear powers and reduce the danger of war.

The debate over the Jackson-Vanik amendment of 1974, for example, which denied most-favored-nation trading status to countries that restricted emigration, including the Soviet Union, embodies this dilemma. On one side of the debate were those who argued that the duty of the United States was to do everything possible to protect the basic human right of emigration; on the other, those who insisted that trade with the Soviet Union was a useful instrument for moderating Moscow's foreign policies.

The drive for independence in the non-Russian republics outside the Baltics presents a second and even more complicated series of choices. The others lack the Baltic peoples' legal and historical claim to Western support. Since their annexation in 1940, the American government has never accepted Lithuania, Latvia, and Estonia as Soviet republics; but when Franklin D. Roosevelt formally recognized the Soviet Union in 1933, the United States implicitly acknowledged the other republics (with the exception of Moldova, which the USSR also seized in 1940) as part of the Soviet state.

Closer inspection, however, reveals this distinction to be a weak basis for the West to decide which claims of independence to support. The republic of Georgia, for example, was part of the Soviet Union in 1933 because the Bolsheviks conquered it in 1921. But Georgia had proclaimed its independence in 1920, and the RSFSR had signed a treaty affirming that independence; 22 foreign countries had also recognized it. In the 1920s, the Baltic peoples were fortunate in that the Red Army was not able to occupy their homelands; the Georgians were not as fortunate. It hardly seems fair to reject Georgia's claims to independence because of this 70-year-old piece of geopolitical bad luck.

Not all the non-Russian republics were unlucky in precisely the way Georgia was, and some came under Russian rule much earlier, but no non-Russian part of the Soviet Union chose its status entirely voluntarily.

Yet, these peoples' claims of sovereignty and declarations of independence contradict a widely honored postwar international principle: the sanctity of existing borders almost regardless of their origins. Governments of every political stripe have feared that abandoning this principle would open the way for endless controversy and even massive violence—to which they themselves might fall victim.

In the Soviet Union, abandoning the existing governing arrangements—even though they were imposed by the imperial expansion of the Romanov dynasty and modified, often arbitrarily and even cruelly, by the communists—would lead to a series of potentially explosive questions.

It would certainly raise the question of who deserves independence, an issue that is bound to be contentious. Gorbachev has already made clear his determination to resist all independence movements, while republics such as the Ukraine may well prove to be divided on this matter.

The question of independence, even if it could be answered to general satisfaction, would raise yet another: Where should the borders be drawn between and among the new independent states? Russia would claim the largely Russian northern part of Kazakhstan, a position that the Kazakhs would not accept. The status of Nagorno-Karabakh has already provoked bloodshed. Other countries could become involved. Ethnic Azerbaijanis live both in the Soviet republic of Azerbaijan and in northern Iran. The international border that divides them is at best artificial. The redrawing of Soviet borders could call into question the line of division between Romania and Hungary, for example, or the Oder-Neisse line, which separates Germany from Poland.

Setting national borders in a way that satisfies all nations and all peoples is no more possible now than it was after World War I, when the most thorough rearrangement in history of the map of Europe took place.

Even if new borders could be decided with minimal dissatisfaction, the question of the status of minorities within the new
states would remain. Ethnic Russians living in Georgia, for example, can move to the RSFSR. For the Abkhazians and Osetins,
however, what is now the Georgian republic is the site of their
ancestral homes. Because they are less numerous than the Georgians, they cannot hope to control the entire republic. Thus,
even as the Georgians demand independence from the Russians,
the Abkhazians and Osetins agitate for freedom from Georgia.
These smaller peoples accuse the Georgians of treating them as
badly as the Georgians claim they are being treated by the Russians. Among the dozens of ethnic groups in the Soviet Union,
many have similar grievances and aspirations.

This second set of issues that the disintegration of the Soviet
state raises will pose two questions of policy for the United States
and the West: which claims to independence to support, and
what steps to take to protect the rights of the many minorities
that are bound to be frustrated by whatever political arrangements emerge from the Soviet Union.

Although the choices the West makes in response to these
issues will be difficult, they may, in the end, be largely academic.
Even if Western governments conclude that they would prefer to
see the Soviet Union preserved in some form, it may well be that
nothing they—or anyone—can do will keep it together. The
continuing collapse of the country could produce far more instability than has occurred thus far, and that could, in turn, present
the West with a third set of issues. The nations of Western
Europe could find themselves flooded with immigrants from the
western republics of the Soviet Union. The West would then have
to either try to absorb millions of people for whom it is not
prepared or, in effect, reconstruct the Iron Curtain.

There is another, even more dangerous possibility. The rise
of nations and nationalism has already generated violence, which
could grow and spread until it becomes a civil war. The national
question has already drawn the Soviet army further into the
political arena than at any time since 1917. A number of its
officers have expressed vehement sentiments in favor of preserving the Union, as well as outrage at the large-scale avoidance

of military service in the non-Russian republics, particularly the Baltics. For their part, many non-Russians see the army as an instrument of both national and personal oppression—the ultimate guarantor of Moscow's authority, as well as an organization in which Russians routinely abuse non-Russian conscripts.

In the event of civil war, the West would have to be concerned about the possibility that the violence would spill over the borders of the Soviet Union into other countries, such as Poland or Turkey. There would also and inevitably be grave concerns about the control of the thousands of nuclear weapons scattered throughout the country.

Nationalist turmoil may, finally, give rise, as Azrael warns, to one or more forms of political extremism in the Soviet Union, which could make the country as dangerous to its neighbors as it was during the long years of the Cold War.

Amid all the uncertainties surrounding the future of the Soviet Union one thing may be safely predicted: nationalism will not disappear. The previous outbreak of nationalist activity, following the 1917 revolution, was ruthlessly suppressed by the communists—along with all other forms of independent political activity. A crackdown of comparable and perhaps even greater brutality would be required to silence all the voices throughout the country now calling for sovereignty and independence. While a return to the terror and mass killings of the first three and one-half decades of communist rule is not impossible, neither is it likely.

Such an outcome is unlikely in part because the last time it occurred, it was undertaken by people acting in the name of an ideology in which they believed, circumstances that cannot easily be re-created now. Moreover, nationalism is more potent now not only because no alternative focus of political allegiance exists and because Soviet rule unintentionally nurtured nationalist feeling, but also because nationalism has achieved an exalted international political status. It has come to be accepted as the normal basis of governance the world over. National self-determination has consequently come to be seen as one of the basic rights of any people.

There is, of course, no universally accepted test for determining just which groups qualify as nations and therefore deserve their own state. In practice, that question is inevitably decided by how much political support and military power a group can muster. But because nationalism is so widely considered legitimate, nationalist claims are useful political tools. When self-proclaimed nations talk, the world listens. In the 1990s, the surest way to get a hearing for any demand—whether for resources, recognition, or territory—is to pose that demand in national terms. Social groups living in the Soviet Union therefore have strong incentives to proclaim themselves nations, the better to get what they want.

Thus the rise of nations in the Soviet Union will continue. It will preoccupy whoever holds power in Moscow. It will influence the political, economic, and social relations among Russians and their non-Russian neighbors. And it will shape Western and American policy toward the peoples and the governments of the large stretch of Eurasia that is now constituted as the Union of Soviet Socialist Republics for the indefinite future, well into the 21st century.

2

RUSSIAN-SOVIET NATIONALITY POLICY AND FOREIGN POLICY: A HISTORICAL OVERVIEW OF THE LINKAGE BETWEEN THEM

Sergei Maksudov & William Taubman

This chapter concerns the impact of relations between Russians and non-Russians on other countries, both before 1917 and since then, and the impact of the outside world on Russian–non-Russian relations in both the tsarist and the Soviet periods. Our topic has not often been addressed in Russian and Soviet studies.[1] Truth to tell, it has not been considered very important until quite recently. Today, the potential breakup of the USSR has focused outside attention on non-Russian nationalities. But even today, it is difficult to recall instances in which Russian–non-Russian relations substantially affected tsarist or Soviet foreign policy, or vice versa. In fact, we shall argue, quite a few such cases have occurred, and they add up to patterns that are not just striking, but also extremely instructive for our time.

Central to these patterns is the existence of empire, a concept that embraces relations between Russians and non-Russians, and foreign relations, as well. With the rise of both the tsarist and the Soviet empires came foreign expansion and heightened control over subject peoples at home. Imperial decay, on the other hand, has meant retreat abroad and new possibilities for non-Russian nationalities within the empire. These two patterns are logical and familiar, but less obvious ones are likewise discernible. Under both the tsars and the Soviets, the growth of empire had the unintended effect of fostering a sense of nationalism on the part of subject nationalities. Such nationalities reacted negatively to dominant Russian nationalism but, in the nineteenth century, they also learned from Russians and

15

other Europeans what it meant to be a modern nation. The tsars' Soviet successors went so far as to provide their "captive nations" with such concrete prerequisites of nationhood as republic status, governmental institutions, an industrial base, and an educated populace.

Imperial decay would seem to open the way to separatism and even potential independence for non-Russian nationalities. But before 1917 such separatism encountered resistance from rulers of the old empire and from champions of a potential new empire, and the same is true today. Russians were the dominant nation in the tsarist era and have remained so throughout the Soviet period, but their nationalism, too, has been subordinate to a larger imperial idea. As each empire disintegrated, the specter of a new, more narrowly Russian empire arose to threaten the hopes of non-Russian peoples.

In both contexts, outside powers played an important role in the rise and fall of the empire, sometimes as victims, sometimes as beneficiaries, almost always as watchful, worried observers. As sometime rivals of the empire, Western powers might have been expected to champion the subversive cause of non-Russian nationalities. Instead, they have often taken their overriding interest to be stability, and so supported either the existing government or its would-be Russian imperial replacement as a matter of realpolitik.

The notion of empire, so central to our argument, must itself be disassembled. Both the tsarist and the Soviet empires rested on three main pillars, but these were different in each period. Under the tsars, these pillars were orthodoxy, autocracy, and *narodnost* (national spirit), to use the terms employed by nineteenth-century statesman Count Uvarov. During the Soviet period, the pillars have been ideology, dictatorship, and nationalism. Moreover, the history of each empire can be divided into subperiods that correspond to each element of the trinity. Our point is not that each pillar gave way to the next, but that each supplemented those that preceded it, at first reinforcing the empire, but ultimately weakening it when the nationalist pillar began to work at cross purposes with the others.

It was thus relatively late in the imperial day that Russian nationalism itself became the main buttress of the empires. Before that, what held them together at home and animated their dealings with outsiders was orthodoxy and autocracy in the first instance, and ideology and dictatorship in the second. But besides buttressing empire, Russian nationalism was bound to undermine it, both because it stood in potential opposition to the statist imperial idea and because it provoked answering non-Russian nationalisms in a multinational domain.

When empires collapse, the question becomes, What next? The years 1917 and 1991 illustrate remarkably similar, but also significantly different, outcomes. After examining the linkage between nationality policy and foreign policy in the tsarist and Soviet periods, we will consider the present and future in the light of 1917. First, however, two comments are in order concerning our decision to give equal time to both empires.

In 1985, one might have relegated the pre-1917 era to a brief prefatory survey on the grounds that it was of historical interest only. Today, we will argue, the tsarist period, and particularly the crucial year 1917, seem no less—and in some ways more—relevant than the Soviet period for understanding the current situation.

Yet, pairing the tsarist and Soviet empires in this chapter raises the question of how similar they actually are. Is the Soviet empire simply the tsarist domain under a new name, that is the Soviet Union? Or is it, as Aleksandr Solzhenitsyn has insisted, a kind of imperial Moloch that demanded and received blood sacrifices from all its nations, and especially from the Russian nation?[2] Obviously, this difference of interpretation goes very deep. It is part of the Westernizer versus Slavophile dispute as to whether the USSR is best understood as an extension of traditional Russian autocracy and political culture (the Westernizer position) or as the imposition onto Russia of a Western (i.e., Marxist) form of political organization.

In our view, both empires were more imperial than Russian, even in their last, Russian nationalist phases. Both empires exploited Russian nationalism (which one might therefore call imperial or statist nationalism) more than Russian nationalism exploited empire. Needless to say, these differences are impossible to measure and extremely difficult to estimate. But we agree with Roman Szporluk, who contends that the Russian "empire never became a Russian nation-state." Szporluk accepts Ladis K. D. Kristof's "notion of a discrepancy or conflict between the 'state idea' of the imperial regime and the 'national idea' of the Russians," a difference captured in the "distinction between *russkii* and *rossiiskii,* between what pertains to the (Great) Russian people and what to All-the-'Russias.'" As Kristof points out, the tsarist empire's formal name was *Rossiiskaia Imperiia,* not *Russkaia Imperiia,* and the tsar was the *vserossiiski imperator.*[3]

This distinction between the imperial and the Russian idea was crucial in 1917 and is so again today. When the tsarist regime collapsed, even liberal Russian nationalists like Paul Milyukov hoped to retain, or even expand, the empire. In 1991, by contrast, for perhaps the first time ever, Russian nationalism has separated itself from, and in some cases even turned against, the idea of empire, thus opening up the possibility of a nonimperial outcome this time around.

THE TSARIST EMPIRE AND ITS PILLARS

The Russian empire took shape even before the Russian nation did, or at least in parallel with it. In that sense, Russians have never lived in a state that was anything *but* an empire. As a result, the borders of that empire have always felt natural and inevitable, even to those Russians who have preached isolationism. For example, when Solzhenitsyn calls upon Russians to abandon the non-Slavic portions of the USSR and occupy themselves with assimilating their own realm, he includes in the Russian heartland areas that were annexed to the empire over the course of the last century or so, like the Amur region and northern Kazakhstan (not to mention Königsberg, southern Sakhalin, Tuva, and parts of Finland).[4]

Another attribute of both Russian and Soviet empires worth noting at the start is that summarized in V. O. Kliuchevskii's famous aphorism: "The state swelled, and the people shrank."[5] In a paper about the nationality issue, we should say all peoples,

Russian and non-Russian, withered under the weight of the despotic state.

Yet, despite these continuities across each imperial era, the history of both the Russian and the Soviet empires can indeed be divided into periods that correspond to the trinity of orthodoxy, autocracy, and nationality.

First Pillar: Orthodoxy

Let us begin, as Count Uvarov did, with Russian orthodoxy. The period we have in mind lasted from the christening of Rus at the end of the tenth century to the fifteenth century overthrow of the Mongol rule by Ivan III. It was during this time that the consolidation of the eastern Slavonic tribes took place, as well as their intermixing with Finnic peoples, their temporary subjugation by the Mongols, and their eventual subordination to a Moscow state.

All these peoples inhabited a region united by religion. Orthodoxy demarcated the boundaries of the Russian state and legitimated its pretensions to further territory in the West then belonging to Lithuania but populated by people professing a belief in orthodoxy. Religion formed the basis for distinguishing natives from infidels, or *inovertsy* (adherents of a foreign creed). Orthodoxy justified designating Moscow as the chosen state, the heir to Byzantium, the Third Rome.

The term "nationality" in its modern meaning did not exist in this period.[6] Greeks were the original carriers of what became Russian orthodoxy, whose texts were written in Old Church Slavonic (really south Slavic), a language far removed from spoken Russian. Ironically, the Mongols protected orthodoxy during their rule. Orthodoxy was the primary prerequisite for inclusion in the Russian ruling class, whether as a boyar or as a member of the *dvoriane* (nobility). Even the Tatar *murzy* (hereditary military elite) were included in the Muscovite aristocracy once the Mongols were defeated, as were indigenous leaders of Turkic and Finnic tribes such as the *chuvash* and *mordvy*. Tatars settled whole regions of the country, such as the Kasimovskii Principality on the Oka. Because their devotion to the Muscovite prince was problematic, since the prince's external enemies were also Tatars, orthodoxy served as a supplementary guarantee of their loyalty. Likewise, orthodoxy played a role in defending against German incursions in the Baltic area, and in gaining the support of many Lithuanian boyars who entered the service of Muscovite princes.[7]

Second Pillar: Autocracy

The Russian word for autocracy, *samoderzhavie*, is composed of two elements—*samoderzhets*, or emperor, and *derzhavie*, which connotes a state or empire with power centralized in the head of that state. The first Russian to openly declare his state an autocracy, and himself tsar and inheritor of both Byzantium and the Golden Horde, was Ivan IV (the Terrible). Under his reign, Russia became a multinational state encompassing vast territories, both along the Volga and extending into Siberia, with Finnish and Tatar populations. It was on the basis of *both* orthodoxy and autocracy (even more than Russian nationality, let alone Russian nationalism) that the Russian empire maintained itself while expanding to the east, west, and south, until roughly the middle of the nineteenth century.

Constantinople having fallen to the Turks in 1453, by the sixteenth century the Muscovite state considered itself not simply orthodox, but the only true orthodox domain. This sense led Moscow to create its own patriarchate in 1589, thus severing the umbilical cord connecting it to Byzantium. Orthodoxy was now a Russian religion. Simultaneously, the character of the state itself changed. The power of the Muscovite prince became both unlimited and hereditary, and to his title Sovereign of All Russia was added Tsar of Kazan, Astrakhan, and so on. Moreover, in a way that foreshadowed later conflicts when nationalism rather than orthodoxy or autocracy fueled Russian expansionism, the sixteenth-century annexation of the Tatar domains of Kazan and Astrakhan sparked a quarrel between Moscow and Turkey. The latter laid claim to Kazan and Astrakhan in the name of its Muslim population; the Crimean khan also considered these lands to be his.

During the Time of Troubles, at the beginning of the seventeenth century, neighboring states and non-Russian peoples increased their influence over the affairs of the Russian state. Tatars and Lithuanians had played a role in the struggle for the Muscovite throne in the fifteenth century; Poles and Don Cossacks played a similar part at the beginning of the seventeenth century. Among pretenders to the throne during this period were notable boyar dynasts (Godunovs and Shuiskiis) and the Polish impostor Vladislav, who would have converted to orthodoxy if he had become the Russian tsar. At the same time, a Russian nationalist element made its appearance in the form of Russian merchants of the northern cities who dispatched the irregulars of Minin and Pozharskii. But if some urban dwellers supported the notion of a *national* autocracy, ordinary people (including peasants and Cossacks) viewed such an autocracy as their archenemy—witness the later rebellions at the periphery by the Cossacks of Stenka Razin, and the followers of the Cossack Pugachev, who proclaimed himself Peter IV, thus winning the support of many non-Russian peoples along the Volga, including the Bashkirs.[8]

Particularly revealing (of the not yet fully Russian character of the Russian empire in these years) was the nationality of those who carried out Russian imperial diplomacy. According to Friedrich Engels, whose summary of the situation was later to evoke the wrath of that non-Russian but extremely pro-Russian tsar Joseph Stalin:

> The external policy of Russia is unquestionably that area in which tsarism has been most powerful. Russian diplomacy formed a kind of new Jesuit order, quite powerful enough to overcome even the Tsar's whims and put a stop, within its own sphere, to the widespread corruption that surrounded it. In the beginning, this order was recruited mainly from foreigners: Corsicans such as Pozzo de Borgo, Germans like Nesselrode, and Baltic Germans such as Liven. The very founder of the order, Catherine II [1729–1796], was a foreigner herself. To this very day [1890] only one pure-blooded Russian, Gorchakov, has occupied the highest post in the order. And his successor [N. K. Giers] once again carries a foreign name.
>
> It is this secret society, recruited mostly from foreign aristocrats, that has lifted the Russian state to its present position of power. . . . It has accomplished more than all the Russian armies in expanding the borders of Russia from the Dniepr and the Dvina beyond the Vistula to the Prut, the Danube and the Black Sea, from the Don and the Volga to the Caucasus and to the sources of the *Amu Darya* and the *Syr Darya*. It has rendered Russia great and

powerful and fearsome, and has opened its path toward world domination.[9]

Third Pillar: Nationality

The idea of the Russian people as a chosen imperial people—a people with a mission to bring religious orthodoxy to the world, to support the principle of autocracy, and to unite various Slavic and non-Slavic peoples—developed during the nineteenth century, first in educated society and then within the ruling class itself. The eventual result of this self-conception was to complicate nationality relations within the empire and to provoke a differentiated Western response to various non-Russian peoples. Western powers had more sympathy for some non-Russians than others. What we now call human rights considerations conflicted with geopolitical aims—with the need to keep the tsarist empire in business as a counterweight to others, but also with the need to keep the Ottoman empire going to check the Russians.

The Russian national idea developed gradually. But by 1839, when the Marquis de Custine visited Russia, Nicholas I had already ordered that Russian be spoken at the court (hence ladies of high station learned a few Russian phrases so that they could be heard to exchange them when the tsar passed by). Nicholas I told Custine that he was a champion of autocracy partly because it was in accord with the temper of the nation. The tsar lamented to Custine how difficult it was for him to also serve as the constitutional monarch of Poland.[10]

In fact, Nicholas not only ceased to recognize the Polish constitution, he suppressed the Polish rebellion of 1830–1831 and dispatched many Poles to Siberia. Protests arose in France and England, and Russia moved toward an alliance with the conservative monarchies of Austria and Prussia. Meanwhile, Polish revolutionaries who had fled Warsaw to Western capitals "were very successful, particularly among liberal circles, in building a picture of tsarist Russia as the embodiment of all that was reprehensible and reactionary in politics."[11] In a sense, then, we have here an early case in which relations between nationally self-conscious Russians and non-Russians (in this case, Poles) adversely affected Russia's standing in other countries. A somewhat similar case involved the Caucasian mountaineer leader Shamil, whose long and fierce resistance to Russian rule complicated Russian relations with Persia and Turkey.[12]

The development of Slavophilism toward the middle of the nineteenth century ultimately had a similar effect. Slavophiles believed that the Russian people had taken their own historical path (in response to the dictates of orthodoxy and the Russian soul) and ought not imitate the West. Their goal, the unification of all Slavic peoples, translated in political terms into a Slavic war of liberation against Turkey. Of course, Slavophilism alone did not trigger such warfare. The Slavophile cast of mind combined with the Russian state's longstanding aspiration to seize Constantinople to produce the Crimean War of 1853. And that, in turn, brought about the English and French intervention that resulted in Russia's crushing defeat.

Previously, those same European powers had long supported Russia in its wars with Turkey; even England had fought alongside Russia to defeat the Turkish fleet in 1828. But the later weakening of Turkey, combined with the outward thrust of an increasingly self-consciously Russian empire, evoked the alarm of many European statesmen, among them Benjamin Disraeli.[13]

In the aftermath of the Crimean War, the arrow linking the nationality issue with foreign relations began to point the other way—that is, from outside the empire back into it. The movement toward domestic reform that resulted from the devastating Crimean War defeat did not actually address Russians' relations with non-Russians; rather, it focused on the need to free Russia's own serfs and thus end its backwardness. But in the long run, the reforms of the 1860s would allow space for non-Russians as well as Russians to organize to defend their interests. In the short run, it was (once again) the Poles who rose in rebellion, in 1863, receiving moral support, but not concrete assistance, from England and France. According to Barbara Jelavich, "it was . . . undoubtedly the Polish insurrection that broke decisively the ties between Paris and St. Petersburg," ties that had been reestablished since the Crimean War (and would be resurrected in the 1890s with the help of a big French loan).[14] Having crushed the rebellion, Russia proceeded to incorporate the Kingdom of

Poland into Russia itself and apply the policy of Russification to other non-Russian areas of the empire, as well.

Later still in the nineteenth century, what earlier could have been called Russian national self-consciousness gradually turned into out-and-out nationalism. Moreover, the regime's attempt to base itself on an imperial Russian nation antagonized other non-Russian nationalities. It was partly in response to intensified Russification that nationalist movements in non-Russian areas began to demand greater freedom and independence. If the Russians had rights and privileges as a people, why should others not have such rights and privileges? Yet, the government denied Ukrainians, Balts, and Poles the right to study in their own languages in upper school grades and in higher educational institutions. Nationalist movements in support of these non-Russian peoples developed in neighboring countries, prompting the Russian government to try to prevent its neighbors from encouraging anti-Russian feeling within Russia itself. In Lvov, for example, then called Lemburg in the Austro-Hungarian empire, Ukrainian scholars published books and journals in Ukrainian, while the tsarist government subsidized publication of the pro-Russian newspaper *Slovo*. Austro-Hungarian Galicia was so rife with activity by Ukrainian nationalists (led by Professor M. S. Grushevskii, who would head the Central Ukrainian Rada in 1917) that it was known as the Piedmont of the Ukraine.

Similar tensions arose in the Asian part of the empire. In its effort to allot sufficient land to liberated Russian peasants, the government seized millions of acres from Kazakh and Kirghiz nomads as part of the Stolypin reforms. The result in 1916 was to provoke local uprisings; the flight of refugees to China, Iran, and Afghanistan; and border tensions with these countries. In bloody clashes in Turkestan, Russians and Kazakhs died in large numbers; afterward, Russians began to flee back to Russia.

Even farther to the east, Russia was building the railroad to China and occupying northern parts of Manchuria. In a sense, this was "straightforward" imperial behavior, but it was accompanied in the press by widespread nationalist and racist propaganda about the "yellow peril" that played no small role in setting the stage for the Russo-Japanese War.

Finally, there was the "Jewish question." Ever since the eighteenth century, Jews had been prohibited from living in purely Russian *gubernias,* and under Nicholas I, their sons had been forcibly baptized and taken into the army for 25-year terms. But it was Alexander III who reduced the Pale of Settlement (forbidding Jews to live outside cities and small towns); introduced quotas in state high schools (Jews were to constitute no more than 3 percent of the students); exiled Jews from Moscow, where they had been permitted to live since 1865; and forbade them to take part in local government. When bloody pogroms occurred in 1881 and 1882, the government sympathized with accusations that Jews were engaging in ritual killings in the Ukraine. It is ironic but revealing that the number of pogroms sharply increased in the immediate aftermath of the tsar's October Manifesto of 1905, offering greater freedom to society. As in the late 1980s, partial political liberalization opened the door to unofficial anti-Semites who interpreted freedom to mean the freedom to beat up Jews. The extreme nationalist Union of the Russian People, which arose in 1905, has its contemporary counterpart in the ultra-nationalist, anti-Semitic society, *Pamyat* (memory).

Coming on top of official government restrictions, this anti-Jewish violence led to massive Jewish emigration (amounting to about 2 million people) to America and, eventually, to tensions between Russia and the United States. According to John Lewis Gaddis, Americans were offended in part by the discrimination to which American Jews were subject while traveling in Russia, but also by what they regarded as "an outrage against humanity." After quiet efforts failed to persuade the Russian government to change its policies, American Jewish organizations got the White House to issue official protests and, finally in 1911, unilaterally to abrogate a Russian-American commercial treaty dating back to 1832. If all this reminds one of similar American efforts in the 1970s, so should the result: abrogation of the treaty failed to create the intended effect; the attempt to interfere brought about an anti-American backlash, especially in extreme Russian nationalist circles; and the Jews' situation further deteriorated as the result of new reprisals.[15]

These, then, are some examples of how increased Russian nationalism poisoned both nationality relations within the empire and the empire's relations with other countries. Moreover, as both sorts of tensions rose, they heightened Russian nationalism itself, which, after the 1905 revolution, several radical nationalist, chauvinist parties (such as the Union of the Russian People and the All-Russian National Union) represented in the new Duma.

On the eve of World War I, Russia's strength seemed substantial. The empire was far-flung and had millions of men under arms. Yet it was rotting at the core. Historians who have debated whether Russia could have survived and even prospered in the absence of world war have concentrated on the country's political and economic condition.[16] But for our purposes the issue is the impact of nationality relations. National and ethnic enmities not only were beginning to boil within the empire, but were contributing to international tensions, as well. Among the causes of World War I were territorial and other concrete issues. But these were part of a complex web of tensions and miscalculations to which the empire's increasingly Russian sense of itself made no small contribution.

As for the war, it aggravated Russian relations with yet another non-Russian nationality—the Germans. Anti-German speeches and pogroms were followed by the arrest and exile of Russian citizens of German background—as well as of Jews, who were regarded as German sympathizers. On the other hand, Czechs and Serbs captured along with other soldiers of the Austro-Hungarian empire were welcomed as brother Slavs and encouraged to form a fighting corps of their own.

Looking back on the tsarist history we have briefly summarized, we can think of no better epitaph than that offered by the tsarist statesman Sergei Witte:

> For decades, our policy has been founded on a basic mistake: we still haven't realized that ever since the time of Peter the Great and Catherine the Great there has been no such thing as Russia; only a Russian empire. When nearly 35 percent of the population consists of *inorodtsy* [non-Russians] (and the Russians themselves are divided into Great Russians, Little Russians, and White Russians), it is impossible to conduct a twentieth century policy that ignores that all-important fact, that ignores the national characteristics—reli-

gion, language, and so forth—of other nationalities that are part of the Russian empire.[17]

We would add only that the Western powers duplicated the error of Russian policy by treating Russia as a unitary empire. They referred to it as a prison house of peoples, but they seemed to care little about those imprisoned in it, with the partial exception of Poles, Finns, and Jews.

THE SOVIET EMPIRE AND ITS PILLARS

If Russian nationalism was the last base and refuge of the tsarist regime, the revolutionary year of 1917 blew up that base while the civil war destroyed or exiled its leading champions. Ultimately, new sorts of nationalisms, such as National Bolshevism, would emerge. But in the meantime, virtually all the non-Russian areas, all the *inorodtsy*, grasped for independence, thus contributing in their own way to the Bolshevik victory.

If our aim here were strictly historical, we would now focus on the months between February and October 1917. But since we want to compare that year with the era of perestroika and glasnost, we will skip past 1917 for the moment, and proceed instead to examine the linkage between nationality policy and foreign policy in the Soviet period.

First Pillar: Ideology

The first pillar of the Soviet empire was ideology. Ideology animated the process of organizing relations among nationalities inside Bolshevik Russia and shaped relations with other countries. In both realms, ideology created conflict; moreover, the two sorts of conflict intertwined. Of course, the new Soviet regime had economic and security interests, too, especially during a time of world war, civil war, and outside intervention. And warmed-over Russian imperial nationalism likewise played a part. For example, Lenin reasserted Russian rights to the Chinese Eastern Railroad even as he repudiated tsarist debts to capitalist states. According to an authoritative Soviet history, the railroad was "built with funds taken by the tsarist government from its taxpayers, that is, from the Russian people."[18]

Like other political parties that had appeared on the Russian political scene before 1917, the Bolsheviks had no clear or fully worked out program for dealing with the nationality issue. But they developed ideas that were sufficiently realistic and attractive to serve them well. At one level, they proclaimed an internationalist commitment to world revolution. At another, they insisted that the achievement of a world socialist state required not Russia's destruction but its transformation. At yet a third level, they offered independence to non-Russian peoples while at the same time calling on them to unite voluntarily in what would eventually become a worldwide Soviet republic. In sum, they promised non-Russian nationalities equality and independence, but with a catch. They would grant such independence only if it served the cause of socialism as defined by the party—and in the eyes of the party, it did not.

While all these abstract principles were being proclaimed, from the Baltic to the Ukraine, and from the Caucasus to Central Asia, non-Russian nationalities were trying to take their fates into their own hands.[19] Weakened for the time being by war and intervention, the Bolsheviks were in no position to dictate the outcome. It would take several years before they won back key areas of the tsarist patrimony. The fact that White forces in the civil war stood for a Russia whole and united won the Bolsheviks some support among non-Russians. But as early as 1918, Lenin and Stalin ordered the commander of the Red Army in the West to "support with every means possible the provisional Soviet governments and, of course, only the Soviet governments of Latvia, Estonia, the Ukraine, and Lithuania."[20] Communists in non-Russian areas depended on the Red Army to seize power and hold power, and eventually the Red Army got the job done. Everywhere except in Finland, Poland, and the Baltics, separatist efforts were snuffed out. Last to be crushed were the Basmachis, whose desperate resistance to Soviet rule in Kazakhstan and Central Asia lasted for nearly a decade.

How did the process of reestablishing the empire intertwine with the new Bolshevik state's foreign relations? Ideology was not the only factor that complicated those relations. Initially, the course of the war was decisive. Until the Treaty of Brest-Litovsk,

Russia remained at war with the Central Powers. After Brest-Litovsk, it was in effect at war with the Allies, who sought Russia's reentry into World War I. But even before the overall armistice in November 1918, and certainly afterward, the Western powers worried about the Bolsheviks' revolutionary ambitions. In the service of those ambitions, Lenin even tried to reach beyond the border of the former Russian empire. He considered, although did not undertake, armed assistance to the Hungarian Soviet Republic and the German proletariat. Likewise, he considered expeditions to Iranian Azerbaijan and even to India.

Of all the considerations that motivated the Allied powers to intervene in Soviet Russia, a firm commitment to independence for non-Russians was conspicuous by its absence. Instead, the West generally took the side of *Russian* nationalism, at first because it seemed the main bulwark against Bolshevism, but also because, despite the demise of the Hapsburg and Ottoman empires, and despite Woodrow Wilson's talk about national self-determination, the West was not about to force the Russians, whether White or Red, to give up their empire.

The kaleidoscopic pattern of national and international conflict during these years is far too complex to convey here. Suffice it to say that both the Central Powers and the Entente got more deeply involved in relations between Russians and non-Russians than any outside power has since, and that the ebbs and flows of German or Allied armies temporarily determined the outcome of Russian–non-Russian conflict in the Ukraine, the Baltics, and elsewhere.

The Baltic states emerged from the civil war period as independent states partly because they "were on Western Europe's doorstep and the great powers were prepared to support them."[21] On the other hand, the Caucasus was far away. As long as White forces were holding their own in the Caucasus, the Allies preferred to back them rather than local non-Russian nationalists. Even as the White Volunteer Army collapsed in the winter of 1919–1920, the Allies declined the three independent Caucasian republics' request to be placed under League of Nations mandates. The Allied Supreme Council extended de facto recognition to Georgia, Armenia, and Azerbaijan, but failed to back that up with concrete support. The Great Powers' de jure recognition of Georgia came just as the Red Army was about to launch the invasion that would establish Soviet rule.[22] Basmachi resistance in Central Asia, which only General Semyon Budenny's cavalry raids ended, attracted some protest in Turkey, but virtually no attention in the West.

In sum, during the civil war period, the West got its best look yet at the multinational nature of the Russian empire, but it paid relatively little attention and soon seemed to forget entirely what it had seen.

Second Pillar: Dictatorship

Before the civil war was over in 1921, and even more afterward, the Bolsheviks realized that they needed not only revolutionary ideology to build socialism, but a powerful state apparatus—which they euphemistically called a dictatorship of the proletariat, but was in fact a dictatorship of the party and ultimately of its leader. In nationality affairs, the corresponding shift was from a putative community of interests among peoples to a commitment to the unity of the newly powerful Soviet state.

The implications of this change were substantial in both nationality affairs and Soviet foreign relations. But in contrast to developments in the earlier period, the two sets of consequences developed in parallel rather than being intertwined.

In nationality affairs, this second period is marked by Stalin's successful efforts to create an extremely centralized USSR. In foreign affairs, Soviet policy moved along two quite different tracks. On one, it continued to support the world communist movement. On the other, it reestablished relations with neighboring states and proceeded to strengthen its economy, partly in preparation for possible war. Moscow also incorporated Bukhara and Khiva (which until then had been formally independent) and the Far Eastern Republic. The West showed little if any concern about these moves; indeed, the United States in effect facilitated seizure of the Far Eastern Republic by demanding the departure of Japanese troops from the region.

Nationality policy might well have been expected to affect foreign policy in the late 1920s and early 1930s. Claims to the contrary notwithstanding, Stalin's brutal collectivization and the famine that followed were *not* directed primarily against non-Russian peoples, although the losses were particularly great in the Ukraine and Kazakhstan.[23] But the national groups there and elsewhere suffered all the more because Stalin's policies took no account of the differences among them, subjecting them all to the same draconian changes. How did the West react to the damage collectivization and famine had done? Hardly at all.

The Ukrainian famine and the desolation of Kazakhstan received little attention in the West, where questions even arose as to whether such events had actually occurred. Moreover, it was precisely during this time period (in 1933) that the United States recognized the Soviet Union for the first time. Of course, the United States and the other Western democracies had various geopolitical, economic, and other reasons for cultivating decent relations with the USSR. Nor were they the first to have had their view of Russian/Soviet reality obscured by Potemkin villages; that tradition, too, went way back in Russian imperial history. But the fact remains that, with the possible exception of Turkey's reaction to the crushing of the Basmachi rebellion, relations between Russians and non-Russians had minimal impact on the USSR's foreign relations during this second period of Soviet empire.

Third Pillar: Nationalism

This situation was to change during the third period. As early as 1936–1937, Stalin's "chosen state" began to attach highest priority to its "chosen people," to the "older brother" of all the Soviet peoples, the "glorious Russian people." Perhaps the first area of Soviet life to feel the impact of this change was language; with the exception of Georgian and Armenian, all the languages of the Soviet peoples were required to adopt the Cyrillic alphabet in the late 1930s. Likewise, Russian history and culture became obligatory subjects of study. Having become Lenin's successor, Stalin obviously wanted to be, and to be seen as, the successor of Ivan the Terrible and Peter the Great.

Mainly because of World War II, but linked as well with the new preference for Russians over non-Russians, Soviet foreign relations soon had a devastating effect on certain non-Russian nationalities within the USSR. Even before the war, in 1937–1938, the government suspected Soviet citizens of Korean and Chinese extraction (approximately 200,000 in all) of harboring sympathy for Japan and therefore exiled them from the Far East to Central Asia. After Soviet troops occupied the western Ukraine, Belorussia, and the Baltics, it sent hundreds of thousands of Poles and Balts to camps and into exile. Finns, too, the indigenous population of Leningrad Oblast, were resettled. Early in the war, Moscow abolished the Volga German Republic and forcibly resettled its inhabitants in Kazakhstan and Siberia. (To this day, Moscow has not reinstated their autonomous status, either on their former territory or anywhere else.) The government also exiled Tatars from the Crimea and various Muslim peoples (as well as Greeks and Bulgarians) from the Crimea and the Caucasus region. Officially, Moscow accused these peoples of collaboration with the Germans; in fact, their exile was part of preparation for an expected clash with Turkey.

The annexation of the Baltics, Bessarabia, and western portions of the Ukraine and Belorussia was clearly aimed at restoring the Russian empire, even though the government justified these moves ideologically as responses to requests by peoples living on these territories. But the new conquests extended beyond the borders of the old empire. Bukovina had been part of Romania; Uzhgorod, Lvov, and Mukachev were taken from Czechoslovakia, Poland, and Hungary, respectively. Königsberg had been German; southern Sakhalin and the Kuriles, Japanese; and Tuva, an independent territory (near Mongolia), became an autonomous Soviet republic in 1944 without any protest from Moscow's wartime allies. Stalin failed in his attempt to occupy Xinjiang during the late 1930s and northern Iran after the war.

During the war, the invading Germans tried to play on Russian–non-Russian tensions. Nazi ploys included treating Russian and Ukrainian prisoners of war differently (often allowing the latter to return to their homes), forming national military units composed of smaller non-Russian peoples, and, of course, identifying the Bolsheviks with the Jews. Such tactics produced lasting successes only in the Baltics, which had just endured a fresh Soviet occupation. (Latvian and Lithuanian military units fought doggedly against the Red Army even under the most hopeless circumstances.) In the Ukraine, Hitler could not bring himself to offer real national autonomy to the population and was soon arresting nationalist followers of Petlura. Still, before the war was over, hundreds of thousands of citizens (mostly non-Russian) fought against Stalin on the side of the Germans, offering resistance that continued long after the war in the Ukraine and the Baltics.

This is not to say that Soviet antifascist propaganda was exclusively Russian nationalist in nature; it also featured internationalist slogans in response to threats the Nazis posed to non-Russian Soviet peoples. During the war, national churches in Georgia and Armenia received greater freedom, just as the Russian Orthodox church did. Even the Jews were authorized to create the Jewish Antifascist Committee, which sent its leading members to the United States to rally support for the USSR and to collect money. Shortly after the war, of course, some of the same committee members were arrested and accused of espionage.

The postwar glorification of the Russian people assumed ugly and even absurd forms: Russians were declared to have been "main victors" in the war; a variety of scientific discoveries were attributed to them; their history, including its imperial expansion, was proclaimed progressive. Meanwhile, the higher party elite consisted mostly of men of Russian nationality.

After the war, what might be called the internal Soviet empire (i.e., the USSR proper) became part of a larger Soviet imperial system in which the three pillars we have been examining came to support three geographically distinct parts of that system. While Russian nationalism increasingly buttressed Soviet rule within the Soviet Union itself, ideology justified support for communist and revolutionary movements and "progressive states" around the world. Meanwhile, in the realm between the internal empire and the world at large, dictatorship (theoretically justified by ideology) was extended to areas that Soviet troops had occupied (East European countries and Mongolia).

Within this intermediate realm, a variety of important state and party agencies were in effect merged or fused with their Soviet counterparts: military, state security, diplomatic, higher party, and even certain economic organs. This process resembled (and was probably modeled on) that which had taken place in the 1920s when the non-Russian republics were merged with the Russian Soviet Federated Socialist Republic (RSFSR). Yet, rumors and signs to the contrary notwithstanding, Stalin did not proceed to include the people's democracies as new Soviet republics. Ideology could have easily been shown to demand their inclusion in a new "world union." Such a republic might also have facilitated the kind of absolute dictatorial control that Stalin exerted within his internal empire. The main reason for *not* creating new Soviet socialist republics was probably a wish to avoid unnecessarily antagonizing the West. But the rise of Russian nationalism within the USSR militated against it, as well. The Russians' weight and influence within an expanded USSR would have diminished. (Actually, the size, if not the relative weight, of the RSFSR was actually *enhanced* after the war with the inclusion of Königsberg—despite the latter's noncontiguity with the Russian Republic—Sakhalin, and a small part of Finland, Pechenga.)

After the war, various non-Russian nationalities were either favored or disfavored in accordance with the dictates of foreign relations. Ukrainians and Belorussians received the great (but empty) honor of having their republics represented at the United Nations. This was Stalin's way of partly making up for Western predominance in the UN. (In retrospect, the situation is highly paradoxical: What would the Baltics not give today to be represented at the UN? Yet, the Americans opposed Stalin's original suggestion that *all* Soviet republics be represented at Turtle Bay.) On the other hand, Moscow did not allow Armenians a day of remembrance to mark their slaughter by the Turks, lest their Turkish neighbors be alienated. As for the Jews, Stalin declared them cosmopolitans, suspect because they were likely to aid Israel or the United States.

Although the plights of various non-Russian peoples commanded the attention of their conationals outside the USSR, the

Jews were the only ones whose situation would eventually prompt the United States to exert substantial pressure on the Soviet Union (thus repeating in the Soviet period the pattern that obtained toward the end of the Russian empire). With the exception of some special sympathy for Baltic refugees (who, in contrast to other former German war prisoners, were not handed over to the Soviets, on the grounds that the Baltics had not been part of the USSR in 1939), American policies toward the USSR hardly took into account the rest. For example, when the Americans decided not to open a consulate in Kiev in protest against Moscow's Afghan intervention, they gave no consideration to Ukrainian nationalists' view that such a consulate could buttress Ukrainian prestige and facilitate contacts with foreigners.

After Stalin's death, the Soviet empire changed in certain details, but not in essentials. Its external zone—the one characterized by ideological and political influence, but not state control—witnessed a dilution of ideology. The USSR counted a series of authoritarian states (such as Egypt, Iraq, and Syria) among its friends; as long as they were prepared to support Soviet policy and declare themselves to be progressive (which in practice meant being not so much anticapitalist as anti-American), they qualified for political and economic support and even military assistance. The intermediate ring of people's democracies received greater political leeway, and economic and cultural autonomy, while control over the army, the secret police, and key party and state personnel assignments remained in Moscow. When that control was challenged or threatened (in East Germany in 1953, Hungary in 1956, Czechoslovakia in 1968, and Poland in 1980), Moscow used military force to reestablish control.

Within the Soviet Union itself, the Khrushchev and Brezhnev period witnessed a weakening of pressure on non-Russian peoples: Moscow rehabilitated Chechens, Ingush, and Kalmyks, who had been repressed (although it allowed the Crimean Tatars, like the Volga Germans, neither to reestablish their autonomous republic nor to return to their native land); the beginnings of nationalist rebirth appeared in the Ukraine while Pyotr Shelest was party leader there; the regional economic councils that Khrushchev temporarily put in place of centralized ministries offered greater leverage to native elites. But meanwhile, Russian nationalism continued to grow, accompanied by the non-Russian (or even anti-Russian) nationalism of smaller peoples. The tension was visible in cadre policy (which continued to place Russians in high posts in non-Russian republics, but also allowed non-Russian party chieftains, including Sharaf Rashidov of Uzbekistan, Vasily P. Mzhavanadze of Georgia, and Dinmukhamed Kunaev of Kazakhstan, to establish native patronage machines) and language policy. In connection with work on the new 1977 Constitution, the Brezhnev leadership floated the idea of abolishing the republics' constitutional right to self-determination (since, after all, nations themselves were theoretically going to merge, leaving a unified Soviet nation in their wake), but characteristically shrank from taking such a decisive step.

How did these developments in the internal Soviet empire affect Soviet foreign relations, and how were they affected in turn? If (with Adam Ulam) we summarize post-Stalin Soviet foreign policy as a combination of expansionism and coexistence, we can indirectly link both elements to Russian–non-Russian relations. On the one hand, Brezhnev-era Soviet expansionism reflected Moscow's conviction that Western power and resolve were eroding as a result of both external overextension and internal decay. Clearly, this view had ideological roots (as well as some connection to Western reality of the 1970s), but it also reflected some traditional Russian contempt for Western democratic institutions. On the other hand, Moscow moved into Czechoslovakia in 1968 partly to prevent Western ideas from contaminating the Ukraine, and into Afghanistan in 1979 partly out of fear of Muslim fundamentalism in Soviet Central Asia, as well as beyond Soviet borders.

As for coexistence, its influence was evident primarily in Soviet treatment of Jews and Germans, who had powerful protectors in the United States and West Germany, respectively. The ability of both groups to emigrate in substantial numbers depended on pressure from their foreign protectors and, of course, on the willingness of Moscow to respond to that pressure so as to solidify détente. Additionally, in the case of the Jews, one must mention Arab pressure in the opposite direction—namely, to limit Jewish immigration into Israel—as well as the effect of the various Arab-Israeli wars (especially the 1967 war) in inspiring many Soviet Jews to emigrate in the first place.

This linkage between nationality policy and foreign policy is suggestive, but not earth-shaking. Why did the nationality issue within the USSR have so little impact on other countries (and vice versa) during the post-Stalin era? Largely, we suspect, because the "super power" of the Soviet Union deterred non-Russian nationalities from rising in anything like revolt, and outside powers from even thinking of interfering. That "super power" consisted of the ability not only to crush any possible non-Russian rebellions, but to bribe non-Russian peoples (and especially their elites) with relative prosperity, upward social mobility, and increasing de facto autonomy. It also included the ability to hide the potentially explosive problems that did exist, not only from the Western powers, but even from the Soviet leaders themselves.

AFTER THE EMPIRE: 1917 VERSUS 1991

Just as 1917 marked the end of the tsarist empire, the current period seems to portend the demise of its Soviet successor. The similarities between the two eras are remarkable, but key differences make the present moment unique. Briefly comparing these two turning points is a good way to survey the most important features of the national question—and their implications for foreign policy—today.

By 1917, and again by the late 1980s, the first two pillars of empire (orthodoxy and autocracy in the early period, ideology and dictatorship later) had weakened almost beyond recognition; while the third pillar, Russian nationalism, was proving more subversive than supportive.

In both periods, imperial decay opened the way for a rapid upsurge of non-Russian nationalist consciousness. The pattern varied in both periods, with peoples in various regions behaving differently. But as central authority eroded, local authorities took on an increasingly nationalist coloration and played an ever larger role in the Ukraine, Georgia, and elsewhere.

In neither period did the central government act quickly and decisively in response to nationalist unrest. The Provisional Government of 1917 put off the national question until the Constituent Assembly could be called. The USSR Supreme Soviet did likewise in the late 1980s. Nor did any of the political parties that appeared on the scene before or during these periods have a clear idea of how to handle the nationality issue.

Unlike their successors in the late 1980s, non-Russian separatist movements in 1917 did not immediately demand full independence. (The exceptions are Poland and Finland, whose current-day counterparts are the newly free nations of Eastern Europe rather than the Soviet republics themselves.) But the Ukrainians, Latvians, and Poles quickly established national armies, much as peoples in the Caucasus region have done today.

Strife among non-Russian peoples on the periphery broke out in 1917 in some of the same places it has in recent years. Azerbaijanis and Armenians fought then, too, as did Russian settlers and local nationalities in Kazakhstan and Kirghizia.

The parallels even extend to foreign policy. Western attitudes have been ambivalent and motives mixed in both cases. Concern about some non-Russians has been greater than that about others; human rights considerations have again clashed with geopolitical aims. Because the Provisional Government's policy was to continue in World War I on the side of the Entente, the Allies supported the central authorities and tried to ignore the nationality question. The West has been repeating the same pattern recently—that is, preferring to deal with the center—except that this time its goal is not to continue a war but to build on the peaceful initiatives of the Gorbachev leadership.

Despite all these similarities, the current moment is unique. For one thing, non-Russians are more conscious of their national identity, better equipped to pursue it, and more determined than were their counterparts in 1917. Back then, nationalism was essentially an elite, urban phenomenon. Today, non-Russian elites are more numerous, and their nationalism has a mass base. To varying degrees, the non-Russian republics also have an industrial base, as well as a complete set of governmental and other institutions, including an administrative and policy apparatus—most of this obtained, ironically enough, courtesy of Soviet power.

Given these contrasts with 1917, it is not surprising that this time many of the non-Russian peoples are demanding not just autonomy within a larger Russian state but full independence. But the reactions of the imperial center and of Russian nationalists are different, too. As of January 1991, the central government in Moscow was stronger than the 1917 Provisional Government—and it remains fiercely opposed to reconstituting the USSR on a narrowly confederal basis, let alone to presiding over the breakup of the USSR. Today's Russian nationalism presents an even sharper contrast with that of 1917.

Liberal Russians still championed empire in 1917. Compare Paul Milyukov, for example, the leader of the Constitutional Democrats, who refused to renounce tsarist war aims, with Boris Yeltsin, whose newfound liberalism seemingly extends to offering autonomy to non-Russians within the RSFSR. Even Solzhenitsyn's conservative brand of Russian nationalism stops far short of Milyukov's imperial reach, since Solzhenitsyn would include "only" the RSFSR, the Ukraine, and Belorussia (along with parts of Kazakhstan) in a new Russian state.

Of all the differences between 1917 and the present, this rise of a small-Russian, nonimperial nationalism is particularly important, as it poses the prospect, for the first time in history, of a Russian nation-state that would not at the same time be an empire.

But the habit of empire (which, as we have said, extends back to the very dawn of the Russian state) dies hard. To judge by the electoral results of 1989 and 1990, most Russians are weary of empire and are inclined to support those who urge emulating the West European example of cultivating democracy at home. But how deep does such feeling go? And how long is it likely to last, especially as the economic crisis that grips the nation worsens?[24]

For the moment, the three pillars of empire may have given way to new combinations: Gorbachev's trinity amounts to socialism, a strong center, and strong republics; radicals champion liberalism, democracy, and independence. But waiting in the wings are new imperial combinations, such as conservative Russian nationalists' orthodoxy, authoritarianism, and nationality, and the ominous slogan that produced a burst of applause at the first session of the USSR Supreme Soviet in 1989—homeland, great power, and communism.

Millions of Russian settlers currently live in non-Russian republics. By their very presence there, they keep the possibility of empire alive. And if and when they come streaming home, telling tales of abuse and rejection by formerly subject nationalities, they could spark a new round of Russian chauvinism. One reason Russians have grown less chauvinist than non-Russians is that whereas the latter blame the Russians for their nations' plight, Russians have no one except themselves (and, of course, communists and Jews) to blame for theirs. Once they start blaming non-Russians, the results could conceivably be national and ethnic strife on a vast scale, even spilling across Soviet borders into Europe or the Middle East.

That brings us back to Western attitudes and reactions. During the decades since 1917, the nation-state has been accepted, even exalted, as the normal form of political organization in the world. This has created powerful incentives for almost any group to call itself a nation and to claim its own state. If the West has been paying more attention to Russian–non-Russian relations this time than it did in 1917, and has looked with greater sympathy on non-Russian causes, that is largely the result of the new legitimacy of national self-determination.

But two other sorts of considerations (one new and the other very old) cut the other way. The new factor is the West's increased commitment to individual human rights. As the non-Russian nations begin to break free of Soviet imperial rule, they may (or may not) receive Western sympathy. But when they begin to war with each other, and to slaughter ethnic minorities within their own borders, even onetime anti-Soviet Westerners begin to wax nostalgic for the former Pax Sovietica.

States have traditionally been more concerned with geopolitical stability than with human rights. Hence the nineteenth-century Western interest in balancing the Russian and Ottoman empires. Hence the West's preference for White Russians over non-Russians during the post-1917 civil war, and its deference to Stalin and his successors at the expense of their subject nationalities. The prospect today of a bloody breakup of the USSR largely accounts for the West's continuing attachment to a stable, unified (if not necessarily unitary) Soviet state. But in our view, such a state is no longer a real option. Force is probably the only way to arrest the unraveling of the USSR, but force itself will bring on the very civil war it is supposed to prevent, while offering no incentive to solve the economic crisis that underlies much of the ethnic unrest.

If a viable, stable, postcommunist Soviet Union is ever to exist, we believe that the republic governments will have to reconstitute it voluntarily. If we are right, then a concern with stability, as well as with national self-determination, suggests that the West reach out to support and influence all the peoples of the former Soviet empire, Russians and non-Russians alike. Too often in the past, under both tsars and Soviets, the West has rejected empire while at the same time treating with the imperialists. At times, this approach may have been necessary. Today, all the major peoples living on Soviet territory should become subjects of U.S. policy, which should encourage them all to coexist peacefully. Not only their future but ours hinges in large part on how Russians and non-Russians get along.

NOTES

The authors would like to thank Peter Czap, Stephen Jones, and Jane A. Taubman for their helpful suggestions, and participants in the Council on Foreign Relations symposium for their comments and advice.

1. For examples of previous studies, see Adam Ulam, "Russian Nationalism," in Seweryn Bialer, ed., *The Domestic Context of Soviet Foreign Policy* (Boulder, Colo.: Westview Press, 1981), pp. 3–18; Jeremy Azrael, "The 'Nationality Problem' in the USSR," in the same volume, pp. 139–154; Robert Conquest, ed., *The Last Empire: Nationality and the Soviet Future* (Stanford, Calif.: Stanford University Press, 1986); and S. Enders Wimbush, ed., *Soviet Nationalities in Strategic Perspective* (New York: St. Martin's Press, 1985).

2. William Safire refers to the USSR as the Russian empire under a new name in his *New York Times* column "Free the Baltics II," September 13, 1990, p.

A27. Solzhenitsyn's latest tract appears in *Literaturnaya gazeta*, September 18, 1990, pp. 3–6.

3. See Roman Szporluk, "The Imperial Legacy and the Soviet Nationalities Problem," in Lubomyr Hajda and Mark Bessinger, eds., *The Nationalities Factor in Soviet Politics and Society* (Boulder, Colo.: Westview Press, 1990), pp. 2–3. English renders both *russkii* and *rossiskii* as "Russian."

4. The northern Caucasus area, which Solzhenitsyn also would retain, became part of Russia in the nineteenth century.

5. V. O. Kliuchevskii, *Kurs russkoi istorii*, vol. 1 (Moscow: Mysl, 1987), p. 61.

6. However, "identity," which sometimes can get fairly close to nationality, did. On this see John A. Armstrong, *Nations Before Nationalism* (Chapel Hill, N.C.: University of North Carolina Press, 1982).

7. According to Kliuchevskii's calculations, only 33 percent of a late-sixteenth-century listing of 930 noble families were of Great Russian background; 24 percent were from Western Slavic families (Ukrainians, Belorussians, Poles) and Lithuanians; 25 percent were Germans and other West Europeans; 17 percent were Tatars and others from the Volga region; and 1 percent were of unknown descent. See V. O. Kliuchevskii, *Kurs russkoi istorii*, vol. 2 (Moscow: Mysl, 1988), p. 193.

8. The Cossacks came in several varieties. Cossacks from the Don and the Urals were a separate group but part of the Russian population. Zaporozhe Cossacks played a key role in the formation of the Ukraine, constituting its military elite and entering into the Ukrainian nobility.

9. This comment appears in Karl Marx and Friedrich Engels, *Sobranie sochinenii*, vol. 16, pt. 2, p. 6. Stalin's opinion, rendered in his article "O stat'e Engelsa, 'Vneshiaia politika russkogo tsarisma,'" first appeared in *Bolshevik*, no. 9 (1941), p. 2, and is reprinted in *SSSR: Vnutrennie protivorechiia*, no. 15 (1986), p. 247.

10. See George F. Kennan, *The Marquis de Custine and His Russia in 1839* (Princeton, N.J.: Princeton University Press, 1971), pp. 74–75.

11. Barbara Jelavich, *St. Petersburg and Moscow: Tsarist and Soviet Foreign Policy, 1814–1974* (Bloomington, Ind.: Indiana University Press, 1974), p. 99.

12. Ibid., p. 83; and Firuz Kazemzadeh, "Russia and the Middle East," in Ivo J. Lederer, ed., *Russian Foreign Policy* (New Haven, Ct.: Yale University Press, 1962), pp. 490–492.

13. See Jelavich, *St. Petersburg and Moscow*, p. 189.

14. Ibid., p. 143.

15. See John Lewis Gaddis, *Russia, the Soviet Union and the United States: An Interpretive History* (New York: John Wiley and Sons, 1978), pp. 29, 41–46.

16. See Leopold Haimson, "The Problem of Social Stability in Urban Russia, 1905–1917," with comments by Arthur P. Mendel and Theodore H. Von Laue, in *Slavic Review* (December 1964), pp. 619–644, and *Slavic Review* (March 1965), pp. 1–56.

17. Sergei Witte, *Vospominaniia*, vol. 3 (Moscow, 1960), pp. 273–274.

18. *Istoriia vneshei politiki SSSR, 1917–1945* (Moscow: Politizdat, 1970), p. 211.

19. For a short summary of this period, see Bohdan Nahaylo and Victor Swoboda, *Soviet Disunion: A History of the Nationalities Problem in the USSR* (New York: Free Press, 1990), pp. 14–59.

20. V. I. Lenin, *Collected Works*, vol. 28, 4th ed. (Moscow: Progress Publishers, 1965) p. 225.
21. Nahaylo and Swoboda, *Soviet Disunion*, p. 47.
22. See Richard Pipes, *The Formation of the Soviet Union: Communism and Nationalism, 1917–1923* (New York: Atheneum, 1968), pp. 193–241, esp. pp. 216–217. Also see Nahaylo and Swoboda, *Soviet Disunion*, pp. 46–47.
23. See Robert Conquest, *Harvest of Sorrow: Soviet Collectivization and the Terror-Famine* (New York: Oxford University Press, 1986), pp. 299–307; and Sergei Maksudov, *Poteri naseleniia SSSR* (Benson, Vt.: Chalidze Publications, 1989), pp. 159–169.
24. The conservative Russian nationalist journal *Molodaia gvardiia* has affirmed that "seven or eight tenths of the whole Russian empire . . . was opened up and united by the heroic, selfless, highly professional work of the Russian peasant. . . . A second means of Russian-style colonization was the voluntary adhesion to Russia of whole countries such as the Ukraine and Georgia." See Vera Briusova, "Are the Russians to Blame for Everything?" in *Molodaia gvardiia*, no. 5 (1990), p. 249.

3

TOTALITARIAN COLLAPSE, IMPERIAL DISINTEGRATION, AND THE RISE OF THE SOVIET WEST: IMPLICATIONS FOR THE WEST

Alexander J. Motyl

How internationalism led to nationalism

Contrary to widespread perceptions, the nations of the Soviet Union are not so much reawakening as they are being awakened. They are asserting themselves, even to the point of pursuing independence, because perestroika has compelled them to do so. Ironically, therefore, none other than Mikhail Sergeevich Gorbachev, a self-styled proletarian internationalist par excellence, must be considered the father of nationalism in the USSR.

How internationalism led to internationalism

Thanks to Gorbachev, not only is the Soviet totalitarian state disintegrating—a fact that can only be welcomed—but it is doing so chaotically—a development that should be cause for alarm. It is to Gorbachev's credit that he destroyed totalitarianism; it is, alas, to his disrepute that he did so in a manner that will have severe repercussions both for the USSR's successor states and for the fledgling democracies of Eastern Europe, as well as for Western Europe and the United States.

The collapse of totalitarianism has transformed the Sovietized nations into the most viable vehicles of sociopolitical opposition and, thus, into the best hope for post-Soviet consolidation. At the same time, the uncontrolled nature of this collapse will confront these nations with insuperable difficulties that can but abort their efforts at economic and political revival. Whatever the exact form that the ensuing political and economic disarray will take, other states—in particular, those of Europe and North America—will feel its effects in at least three ways. The incapacity of the post-Soviet republics to halt ecological decline will undermine their ability to address environmental issues

44

effectively. Waves of refugees from the continuing chaos of the post-Soviet states will assault their borders and sorely test their commitment to human rights. And as political instability engulfs the republics and confronts the West with painful choices that erode its hopes for unity, their security will be threatened. As I suggest below, the West would do well to forestall such a dismal future *before* euphoria over the end of the Cold War becomes despair over the enormous costs perestroika has imposed on the world.

DETOTALIZING THE SOVIET STATE

In 1985, when Mikhail Gorbachev assumed the mantle of general secretary of the Communist Party, the totalitarian Soviet state monopolized all the public space civil society generally occupies in democratic countries. It was still very much in charge in 1987–1988, when independent political, social, and religious groupings began emerging throughout the Soviet Union. Since then, however, literally everything has changed. The formerly Leviathan state has shriveled, and it has done so with breathtaking rapidity.

Several factors deserve special attention in explaining the collapse of Soviet totalitarianism. First, by destroying Soviet ideology and values, rampant glasnost effectively transformed the Soviet Union into a criminal state. Not surprisingly, close investigation of the all too many blank spots in Soviet history led to repudiation of the entire Soviet experience. As revelations of Stalinist and post-Stalinist crimes against humanity came to light—culminating in the discovery of numerous mass graves containing the mutilated remains of countless workers, peasants, and other "bourgeois enemies of the people"—most Soviet citizens logically concluded that their regime was little different from that of Hitler.

Second, Gorbachev's haphazard economic reforms and assault on the system's only stable political institution—the party— threw the economy into chaos. After all, the command economy functioned, albeit inefficiently, as long as the central bureaucracies determined inputs and outputs and the party possessed the authority to implement their decisions and, thus, to command. Once the powers of central ministries were curtailed and the authority of the party was eroded, while little was done to introduce genuine market mechanisms, the Soviet economy was left with the worst aspects of two competing economic approaches: neither capitalist nor socialist, it could but decay to the point of collapse.

Third, Gorbachev's attempt to create new political institutions under these conditions was certain to result in failure. The quasi-representative bodies—the Congress of People's Deputies, the revamped Supreme Soviet, the presidency—could not possibly assert their authority and establish their legitimacy in circumstances of extreme discord and economic decline. Indeed, Gorbachev's own transformation into an unpopular dictator is the inevitable consequence of his tinkering with totalitarian politics and economics.

Fourth, Gorbachev's willingness to tolerate the emergence of political oppositions amid systemic collapse provided them with the very ideological, economic, and political ammunition they needed to assert themselves above the institutions he had created and those, such as the party, he had weakened. Moreover, the loosening of the party's control over its republican branches left them defenseless against criticism from below, thus forcing them to be responsive to their ethnic constituencies, to adopt increasingly nationalist positions, and, finally, to forge informal coalitions with republican popular fronts against the center.

Two errors—one tactical, the other strategic—account for the chaotic character of Gorbachev's brand of detotalization. The first involves, as he himself has admitted, gross mistakes in policy. Gorbachev wholly underestimated, among many factors, the immense unpopularity of the Communist Party and the extent of national discontent in the republics. As a result, his endorsement of glasnost opened a veritable Pandora's box that quickly transformed the Soviet citizenry's insatiable thirst for knowledge of their past and present into a weapon not of the state, but of society against the state. Glasnost, quite simply, thoroughly delegitimized the party and exposed the Soviet Union as an empire.

G. embarked on radical reform while consolidating power — MISTAKE

Gorbachev's second error, which greatly compounded the first, was to embark on radical reform while consolidating power, a strategic miscalculation that enmeshed his policies in a pair of fatal contradictions. Attempting to pursue reform and power simultaneously, and thereby repudiating the traditional pattern of Soviet succession dynamics, guaranteed failure on both counts. Thus, Gorbachev's struggle against the party negated the possibility of real reform, as only the party was in a position to change the system in a stable and predictable manner. Gorbachev's pursuit of radical reform, meanwhile, made it impossible for him to consolidate control of the party without destroying its authority in the process. In the end, reform could but fail, while the party, the country's only effective political institution for close to 70 years, could but decay. Without the party, Gorbachev's own authority could not extend beyond the Kremlin's walls; without reform, new institutions could not be created, and his legitimacy perforce went into steep decline.

Worse still, Gorbachev also left himself dangerously vulnerable to attacks from those of his opponents ensconced in the very party and state institutions he was attempting to transform. Not surprisingly, such vulnerability repeatedly induced Gorbachev to deny that the deleterious consequences of poorly conceived policies were unintended and, thus, compelled him to embrace developments that were manifestly harmful to perestroika. An excellent example of Gorbachev's unwillingness to distinguish publicly between tactically expedient actions that outflank political opponents and strategically suicidal moves that undermine systemic stability was his enthusiastic support of the miners' strikes of mid-1989. In hailing such popular initiatives, Gorbachev undermined the country's ability to sustain itself and, consequently, to weather the radical reforms promised by perestroika.

The result of Gorbachev's miscalculations is that the detotalization of the Soviet system—a hopeful development that must be welcomed—has occurred chaotically, a dreadful process that cannot be. Such *stikhiinost,* a Russian word that fully captures the uncontrolled character of Gorbachev's misrule, was not inevitable. Although the experience of other communist states suggests that totalitarian systems may not be reformable and that their collapse may be inevitable once reform is initiated, it also illustrates that chaos is avoidable if the process of detotalization is extended and deliberate. The examples of Hungary and China show that substantial sectors of the economy can undergo detotalization in advance of the polity's decay, while that of Poland suggests the possibility of the emergence of a nascent civil society. Nonchaotic detotalization may not save communist states from doom, but it does facilitate the postcommunist transition to democracy and the market by contributing to the creation of the rudimentary social, political, and economic institutions that serve as the base on which genuine civil societies can be constructed. To be sure, even the stable, autonomous, and socially cohesive institutions that healthy civil societies provide do not guarantee functioning democracies and effective markets. Nevertheless, they are a necessary condition of both. Such institutions act as intermediaries between citizens and the state—without which democracies cannot function—and as the guarantee of private property and private enterprise—without which markets are impossible. In contrast, while chaotic detotalization does not exclude the eventual creation of civil society, it does make the process immensely more difficult. As a result, despite the enormous challenges confronting Poland, Czechoslovakia, and Hungary, their experience with prolonged detotalization provides them with an immeasurable lead on the post-Soviet republics, Romania, and Bulgaria.

THE EMERGING QUEST FOR SOVEREIGNTY

One of the wholly unexpected consequences of pell-mell detotalization has been the remarkably rapid collapse of the USSR's East European empire. Although it may be true that Gorbachev and his advisors understood that Soviet hegemony in Poland, Czechoslovakia, Hungary, East Germany, Romania, and Bulgaria was coming to an end, they cannot possibly have desired the ignominious denouement that occurred in late 1989. And yet, such an end was inevitable as uncontrolled detotalization severely delimited the USSR's capacity to project power beyond its borders. Once the illegitimate East European satraps were severed from their lord in Moscow, it was only a matter of time before popular oppositions led by determined elites and frequently charismatic leaders would oust them.

The collapse of communism in the countries of Eastern Europe presages the future of the Soviet republics, as well. Political, economic, social, and ideological chaos has created opportunities for national oppositions to emerge; furthermore, it has literally forced the republics to turn inward as their only defense against a collapsing political and socioeconomic order. The universal rush to sovereignty of all Union republics, several autonomous republics, some regions, and even a few cities is the result not of political culture or of nationalist inclinations—after all, how could it be if even the Chukchi have declared sovereignty?—and it is hardly "mindless," as Gorbachev would have the West believe. Quite the contrary, the quest for sovereignty is the direct result of perestroika. Gorbachev's inability to transform a totalitarian state in an orderly fashion has compelled republics and other administrative units to act in accordance with their interests and, quite rationally, to seek refuge in independence. Swiss bankers would behave no differently. They, too, would have no alternative if they wished to survive in the postperestroika USSR.

Three other factors have galvanized the quest for sovereignty. First, the collapse of Soviet ideology has created an ideological vacuum that ethnicity and religion, two sources of meaning that managed to survive totalitarian assaults relatively intact, rushed to fill. They were especially attractive as substitute systems of meaning, inasmuch as the core of the discredited ideology consisted of an anational entity called the Soviet people who, of course, were fundamentally atheist.

Second, Lenin's policy of creating titular republics endowed with symbolically sovereign statehood actually laid the institutional grounds for opposition to the center. Like the East European people's democracies, the Soviet republics possessed all the trappings of sovereignty, including local bureaucracies, planning organs, foreign ministries, and republican parties, while Belorussia and the Ukraine also were members of a host of international bodies. Once the opportunity to fill these forms with appropriate national content presented itself, the republics were fully equipped to act accordingly.

Finally, the decades-long Soviet persecution of non-Russian dissidents, who represented the vast majority of all Soviet political prisoners, transformed mere defenders of language and culture into ardent nationalists determined to save their nations by divorcing them from the imperial center. Moreover, by incarcerating the dissidents in concentration camps, Moscow effectively helped these nationalists forge transrepublican alliances and refine their anti-Soviet programs, while by releasing them in 1986–1987, it set loose a determined and organized opposition elite on the weakened Soviet body politic.

Because detotalization has spun out of control, Gorbachev has finally succeeded in creating a situation that is truly irreversible. As a result, imperial collapse, the direct consequence of detotalization, can but reach its logical conclusion: some form of independence for all the republics. A pan-Soviet societal consensus is no longer within reach, as social animosities cannot possibly be overcome in the near future. An all-Union economy cannot be revived without accelerating centrifugal forces: a return to the command economy is institutionally impossible, doing nothing would be disastrous, while marketization—in contrast to a functioning market—would only drive the republics further apart. All that is left to hold the Union together is coercion, and as Eduard Shevardnadze's resignation as foreign minister and the halfhearted crackdown in Vilnius and Riga indicate, Gorbachev fully understands that the president's only remaining allies are the forces of "law and order." But even coercion can no longer do the trick. A crackdown would be unlikely to succeed for two reasons. First, there is evidence to suggest that the KGB, the military, and especially the police are beginning to fragment along republican lines. Second, and more important, the degree of anti-Soviet, anticommunist, and anti-imperial sentiment in the non-Russian republics, as well as in Russia itself, is so intense that the inevitable result of a crackdown would be a massive civil war that the forces of a declining center could not win. For better or for worse, the time to have cracked down successfully was no later than 1989. Indeed, one suspects that even the military and the KGB must recognize that a countrywide Tiananmen is no longer in the cards.

STATE-BUILDING AFTER DETOTALIZATION

The post-Soviet republics will have to confront the disastrous legacy of decades of communism, and they will have to do so without the benefit of strong civil societies, stable political institutions, and experienced elites. A comparison with postcolonial Mozambique and Angola is instructive. There, too, imperial collapse left the native populations bereft of resources and facing staggering problems. But unlike the Sovietized nations, which had been traumatized by decades of totalitarian rule, Mozambique and Angola did not face the task of creating market economies and civil societies from scratch. In this sense, their problems, however immense, were fewer and somewhat less complex. Clearly, the fact that both countries are still among the poorest in the world and are still embroiled in civil wars—conditions that obviously are also related to their underdevelopment—does not bode well for the future of the post-Soviet republics.

A glance at the former East Germany may also be worthwhile. The transition to democracy and capitalism in East Germany, a country once routinely touted as socialism's success story, is taking place under conditions that cannot be repeated in Eastern Europe or in the post-Soviet republics. Even East Germany's reunification with West Germany may or may not ensure that the billions of dollars to be pumped in annually will raise its socioeconomic level to one approximating that of the West. Needless to say, neither political annexation, military occupation, nor such massive economic aid is likely to be forthcoming in the case of the post-Soviet republics.

Nevertheless, although the future of the republics looks bleak, grounds for some optimism remain—especially in light of the utter impossibility of the Soviet Union's revival. In contrast to any version of the fragmented Union—which cannot reestablish societal consensus, build civil society, or acquire stable political institutions, for the reasons adduced above—the republics have one enormous asset enabling them to embark on all three tasks. Quite simply, they are the titular homelands of particular nations, and just as the upheavals in Eastern Europe were part and parcel of national revivals, likewise only the Sovietized nations can save the post-Soviet republics.

The nations can do so by serving as ready-made vehicles of consensus, civil society, and political stability. Thus, inasmuch as national identity is rooted in a sense of national community, it automatically provides for a certain amount of societal cohesion. By the same token, national traditions—be they religious, political, or exclusively cultural—can underpin the institutions of an emergent civil society. Finally, national fronts, which enjoy widespread legitimacy in all the republics, can endow the political arena with stability, as well as generate some of the institutions that must come to populate it. Consequently, if stable transitions to democracy and the market are ever to occur in the former USSR, they can—but need not—occur *only* in the republics.

They need not do so precisely because the nation and the institutions it generates can be double-edged swords. Thus, the republics, qua republics, like some of the countries of Eastern Europe, face at least two daunting dilemmas. The fact that distinctly national movements form the base on which multiethnic civil societies must emerge may lead to conflict and competition among ethnic majorities and minorities precisely at a time when ethnic peace is a sine qua non of the building of civil society. At present, the democratic leaders of national movements, such as the Lithuanian Sajudis or the Ukrainian Rukh, have managed to incorporate ethnic minorities into majority movements. It is not too difficult to imagine their replacement with less effective or less restrained individuals. Nor is it unlikely that continued social, political, and economic chaos will increase interethnic strains and conflicts.

Second, pell-mell detotalization has suddenly cast republican popular fronts in roles—as political parties and statebuilders—for which they are singularly unprepared. Social movements are excellent vehicles of popular mobilization or of single-issue politics. Everyday politics, on the other hand, requires professional organizations and nonpartisan institutions that can act as channels for a variety of political forces. Popular fronts are ideally equipped to provide the impetus for such institutions, but unless they eventually dissolve, they can also become barriers to the effectiveness of these same institutions. The role of Solidarity in postcommunist Poland may be instructive in this regard.

To complicate matters, just as republics have few stable social and political institutions, so, too, they lack seasoned and credible political elites. On the one hand, in the post-Soviet republics, as in the East European countries, the ongoing decline of communist parties will eventually result in the call for purges, retribution, and trials of particularly egregious offenders. Decommunization, like de-Nazification, may be morally justified, indeed necessary; yet it is likely to have the most serious consequences for republican political and economic systems. After all, it is by and large only the communists who possess the bureaucratic skills needed to run complex polities and economies. Their removal, however understandable, will both increase social tensions and undermine the effective working of fledgling political systems. On the other hand, not only do most of the writers in charge of popular fronts have no idea of how to create market economies (for which they cannot be faulted, as Western economists are at no less a loss), but the policies they pursue in attempting to make transitions to market systems are likely to result in so much suffering as to undermine their own political status. Triple-digit inflation and unemployment of over 50 percent are a recipe for political disaster, especially for untrained and inexperienced political elites.

Under conditions such as these, when weak elites must make extravagant promises in the face of virtually insoluble problems, the temptation for unscrupulous and disloyal oppositions—be they communists, soldiers, fascists, Nazis, or others—to subvert the democratic process is virtually irresistible. Even if this worst-case scenario does not come to pass, the postcommunist elites of the Sovietized republics—or, for that matter, of Poland, Hungary, Czechoslovakia, Romania, and Bulgaria—almost certainly will be unable to cope with perestroika's deadly consequences.

Ungovernability, political deadlock, and a return to the maximalist politics of the interwar period are likely to result—but with one enormous difference. This time, the political ineffectiveness and instability will be played out on the wreckage of a totalitarian system, whose economic, political, and ideological pathologies will haunt the postcommunist states for decades to come.

ISSUES FOR THE WEST IN THE POST-SOVIET ERA

The republics of the Soviet West—Estonia, Latvia, Lithuania, Belorussia, Moldova, and the Ukraine—will have a significant impact on Eastern Europe, Western Europe, and the United States because of one overriding factor, geographic proximity. Simply put, the Soviet West is about to become the West's backyard. The collapse of the Berlin Wall and the removal of the Iron Curtain have ensured that something in the nature of a two-class European "common home"—one resembling the type of nineteenth-century dwelling occupied by *haute bourgeoisie* and *lumpenproletariat*—will soon become a reality.

Developments in the Soviet West will affect Western states for three additional reasons. First, because the Baltic republics have a special relationship with the United States, which has never recognized their incorporation into the USSR, while the Ukrainians and Belorussians have seats in the United Nations and other international forums, these nations will increasingly voice their grievances, make demands, and curry favor on the world arena. By insinuating themselves into the diplomatic agenda of the international system of states, they will eventually become players, even if minor ones, in a particularly sensitive part of the world.

Second, virtually identical economic systems, common economic problems, and a shared cultural and historical legacy suggest that a new Eastern Europe, incorporating Poland, Hungary, Czechoslovakia, Belorussia, the Ukraine, and Lithuania, will emerge in the near future. As problems of postcommunist and post-Soviet development will be common to all these states, the West will no longer be able to formulate one set of policies for

Poland, Hungary, and Czechoslovakia, and another for the republics.

Finally, most of the republics of the Soviet West have sizable and vocal diasporas in Western Europe, the United States, and Canada, while all have close ties with ethnic cousins in Eastern Europe. Although émigré influence on policymaking has historically been minimal—with the obvious exception of that exercised by American Jewry—it is likely to increase as the post-Soviet republics become more important policy issues for the West.

Because the West cannot possibly isolate itself from the Soviet West, the latter's problems—and they promise to be many—will be our problems. First on the short list is ecology. Environmental destruction in the region will continue unabated for many years, if only because Eastern Europe must increase its reliance on "dirty" coal reserves and unsafe local nuclear energy facilities since Moscow raised its price of oil to world levels in 1991. Western Europe will not be able to ignore such devastation because closer economic ties and transportation links will expose more of the West to the East's pollution, while heightened concern about ecological issues will be frustrated at a time when it is assuming the exalted status of dogma in West European political discourse. Another Chernobyl—a possibility that should not be discounted—would quickly force the European Economic Community (EEC) and the United States to take an immediate interest in the environmental affairs of the East.

The extreme likelihood that both Eastern Europe and the Soviet West will sink to the level of economically marginal countries will lead to massive unemployment and social dislocations, and will undermine political stability. The immediate consequence of such developments will be emigration. As millions of refugees flee westward, Western Europe, the United States, and Canada will have no choice, short of reraising the Iron Curtain, but to accept them. Absorbing millions of former Soviet citizens will be internally disruptive, straining social welfare systems, producing ethnic backlash, and even threatening the democratic consensus. Rejecting them, however, will not only be a crass repudiation of human rights and, indeed, of everything that the West claims to stand for; it will also be externally disruptive, pushing the republics of the Soviet West even deeper into misery.

Most of the dilemmas of Western Europe are likely to be the dilemmas of the United States, as well, only more so. Unlike the West Europeans, who have never made human rights a fundamental part of their foreign policies, Americans will face some wrenching moral choices that will test the depth of their commitment to human rights. Just as Washington's insistence that the USSR permit Soviet Jews freely to emigrate resulted in a closed-door policy once the Kremlin did just that, when millions of non-Jewish economic and political refugees—no doubt including thousands of communist criminals and their collaborators—ask to be admitted, the United States will either have to abandon its moral stance or permit millions of East Europeans to immigrate, at a time of growing social tensions and economic stringency at home.

As disturbing as environmental destruction and refugees are likely to be, the greatest source of difficulty for Eastern Europe, Western Europe, *and* the United States is the high probability of prolonged political instability in the postcommunist states of the Soviet West. Poland, Czechoslovakia, Hungary, and a Romania enjoying increasingly close ties with Moldova would be affected immediately, especially as they are already engaged in seemingly intractable disputes over ethnic minorities. It does not, alas, strain the imagination to conceive of the entire region's reverting to interwar animosities, border conflicts, and military buildups, with the breakdown of democracies in the Soviet West leading to the breakdown of postcommunist democracies in Eastern Europe. Indeed, Václav Havel's request in late 1990 for emergency powers may be a foretaste of things to come.

Even more worrisome, if and when massive instability engulfs the East, it could undermine East-West security arrangements. One cannot discount the possibility that desperate republics may come into possession of nuclear weapons, given that the western border districts are still home to a variety of Soviet military units and armaments. Equally terrifying is the prospect of Russia's reasserting its national honor or asserting its interests by means of military expansion into the Baltics or the Ukraine. Finally, Western negotiations with what remains of the USSR over troop reductions and nuclear disarmament will become immensely more complicated if some five to ten additional actors demand a voice in the process.

The Soviet West's inevitable liberation will thus be profoundly destabilizing for a West that does nothing to cushion the shock. Whether Western Europe can survive as a coherent entity when confronted by such pitiable neighbors is a question well worth pondering, especially in light of the proposition that the division of Europe into two ideologically hostile, economically incompatible, and politically competing halves enjoying the protection of hegemons may have been the necessary condition of the emergence of a unified Western Europe. If so, then the return to multipolarity in Europe may mean that realist logic will reassert itself, that security issues will again come to the fore, and that Western Europe's economic and political unification will remain on paper—especially if, as seems likely, turmoil and instability on Germany's eastern border draws it away from its EEC partners and involves it in the affairs of its neighbors to the east. Of course, international values may have changed and interdependence may have grown to such a degree as to prevent the reassertion of *raison d'état* over the moral imperatives of international community. But because Euro-optimism is such a recent phenomenon and follows, we dare not forget, a Euro-pessimism that seemed equally well-founded, it is at least plausible that the sentiments expressed in the Charter of Paris are, perhaps, Panglossian.

Security will pose the greatest dilemma for the United States. With the end of the Cold War, the United States has emerged as the world's only genuine superpower, a role for which this country is, understandably, utterly unprepared. As the American involvement in the Persian Gulf suggests, the logic of "unipolarity" may force the United States to become the world's sole policeman. Political instability or civil war in the USSR's successor states—be they in the West, the Caucasus, or Central Asia—might require the United States not only to expend scarce resources in Western and Eastern Europe, but also to involve itself even more deeply in the precarious politics of the Middle East. The "peace dividend" is unlikely to be sizable in an increasingly anarchic world dominated by one genuinely great, though apparently declining, power—the United States.

WESTERN POLICY OBJECTIVES

Like it or not, developments in the post-Soviet republics will affect Western Europe and the United States. Indeed, as Europe increasingly becomes a single continent, speaking of the East as if it were remote and removed from the West will be impossible. The question, therefore, is not, Should the West get involved in the problems of the post-Soviet republics? It is, rather, How and to what extent should the West get involved? What policies should it formulate to avert the impending dangers?

The past offers little guidance, as Western policy toward the republics has been virtually nonexistent, while Western interest in and knowledge of the region have been only marginally less so. As Sergei Maksudov & William Taubman demonstrate, except for Western intelligence support of the post–World War II undergrounds in Lithuania and the Ukraine, and Radio Liberty, BBC, and Deutsche Welle broadcasts to the region, the West has always preferred to deal with Moscow, be it as the center of tsarism or as the capital of the first workers' state. Nazi Germany may have been the only exception to this rule, but its policy toward the non-Russians was both temporary and tactical.

Western policy toward Eastern Europe—such as bridge-building—is equally unhelpful as a guide, insofar as national diversity, increased democracy, and greater autonomy, which were the goals of bridge-building, are no longer at issue in the disintegrating empire that is today's USSR. Quite the contrary, the West has an immediate and overriding interest: to minimize instability while recognizing that the empire cannot be revived. Such a pressing goal requires activist policies. Leaving the matter in Gorbachev's hands would surely lead to disaster, as the fate of the Soviet Union is too large a matter for the ruler of the Kremlin to determine on his own.

In an ideal world of limitless resources and limited constraints, the West in general and the United States in particular would adopt some or all of the following measures:

- Pressure Gorbachev to dissolve the Soviet Union immediately and to replace it with a confederation of sovereign states. Gorbachev's insistence on a new Union treaty and his unwillingness to make a clean break with the past are only intensifying resentments, increasing polarization and radicalization, and thereby virtually assuring that the break with Moscow, when it does come, will be as bloody as possible. Forcing Gorbachev's hand now, when he is relatively dependent on Western support, would immediately reduce tensions between and among republics and introduce a greater degree of clarity and sobriety into the calculations of republican political elites. The sooner they begin addressing their pressing problems, the better. The longer they wage a divisive national liberation struggle against Moscow, the greater the resource waste and the polarization of society, the smaller the chances that they will succeed in directing popular energies at the resolution of concrete tasks, and the less likely that they will want to maintain even economic relations with a sovereign Russia. Only a confederation of post-Soviet states, perhaps even headed by a figurehead president residing in Moscow, has any chance of providing a workable structure for republican cooperation on a whole range of security, foreign policy, and economic issues.

- Immediately establish diplomatic relations with the republics of the Soviet West, even if Gorbachev opposes the dissolution of the USSR. If the price of such an intervention in Soviet affairs is Gorbachev's fall from power, then so be it. Surely it is high time for the West to realize that the USSR's current condition is the direct result of his policies. Besides, Boris Yeltsin, who supports republican sovereignty, would be most likely to succeed Gorbachev, and his overall stewardship could not be any worse than Gorbachev's.

- Warn Moscow that the West will respond to the repression of republics and "democrats" with diplomatic and economic sanctions along the lines of those imposed on Iraq after Saddam Hussein's invasion of Kuwait. Civil war in the Soviet Union must be avoided at all costs, and that means deterring the army and the KGB from embarking on something as foolhardy and counterproductive as a countrywide Tiananmen.

- Envelop the republics in as many supranational institutions as possible so as to provide them with stable structures and values for dealing with their problems. This may mean membership in the International Monetary Fund (IMF), and the World Bank, inclusion in the Conference on Security and Cooperation in Europe process, membership in the North Atlantic Treaty Organization, observer status in the EEC, and so on. The exact form of involvement is less important than the inclusion of potentially unstable countries in a stable institutional environment. If international norms are imposed on republican elites, there is at least a chance that they will accept these strictures and avoid violations of human rights, aggressive behavior, and the like. By the same token, by involving these nations in Western institutions, the West would have a greater say in the formulation and implementation of their policies toward, say, ethnic minorities.

  In particular, insist that the United Nations, which has been revitalized as a result of the Persian Gulf crisis, play a prominent role in the affairs of these countries. United Nations assistance—technical, financial, and humanitarian—may have a stabilizing influence on the elites and populations in the region. Such involvement assumes, of course, United Nations membership for the Baltic states, Moldova, Russia, and other post-Soviet republics.

- Encourage, if not indeed compel, all the countries of Eastern Europe and the Soviet West to declare themselves nuclear-free zones and to sign the Nuclear Non-proliferation Treaty, to maintain strict limits on the size of national armies, and to forswear territorial claims on their neighbors.

In return, promise these countries technical, financial, or other forms of material assistance for the rebuilding of their economies.

- Initiate a second Nuremberg, at which the leading representatives of the former communist regimes and their collaborators would stand trial and be sentenced for their crimes against humanity. Only the West has the moral authority and the political clout to engage in such a replay of history. Such an action is both morally imperative and politically expedient, as it would depoliticize the issue of decommunization by internationalizing it. It would minimize the divisiveness that would result from local purges and bloodletting, and enhance the West's moral authority in the region.

- Finally, and most important, provide massive economic aid to the republics. If the democracies are not moved to embark on such a measure for the promotion of human rights and civil liberties, they should at least consider the sobering thought of having to live with ten Mozambiques east of the Oder-Neisse line. Ultimately, only an economic recovery can stem the flood of refugees, stabilize governments, reduce ethnic tensions, and help fledgling democracies survive. The costs of such a second Marshall Plan would, of course, be enormous, but they are unlikely to be any higher than those incurred after the region explodes and costly crisis management becomes imperative. The cost of the American intervention in the Persian Gulf may serve as a reminder of what peacekeeping in Eastern Europe might involve.

Specifically, the IMF, the World Bank, and the European Bank for Reconstruction and Development should provide financial help to all the republics, while the industrial democracies grouped in the Organization for Economic Cooperation and Development should funnel direct developmental assistance at least on the order of their current aid to the Third World. In no circumstances, however, should assistance be forthcoming to the crumbling imperial center in Moscow. Such moneys will inevitably be misused by the central economic ministries, while merely prolonging the misery of a dying empire. Either way, Western resources will be wasted.

FIRST STEP: NO STEP

Of course, the world is not ideal, and Western governments are certain not to respond in this manner. Such massive policy shifts as recommended above usually take place after, and not before, crises occur. An immediately tangible disaster—the functional equivalent of an invasion of Kuwait or a blitzkrieg against Poland—is usually the sufficient condition of policy revolutions, and the Soviet Union has not yet fallen victim to a bloody civil war.

Can nothing, therefore, be done to prevent disaster from occurring? Ongoing efforts to help Eastern Europe, such as those initiated largely by the private sector, are for the most part confined to encouraging entrepreneurship, training elites, and supporting the creation of social and political institutions. These are, of course, all worthwhile measures, but they will not produce significant results in the short term. Building civil societies and stable polities will take decades, while the post-Soviet republics will have only years to address their problems. Indeed, as Poland's recent political travails suggest, even wildly popular postcommunist governments may not have the wherewithal to survive economic shock therapy without lapsing into political demoralization.

What, then, should the West do? While it may be unwilling to recognize Gorbachev's subjects as sovereign, surely the time has come for it to realize both that the emperor's realm is disintegrating and that the West may soon become the largest prop of his remaining authority. If accelerating imperial dissolution is a nonstarter for policymakers, then reverting to the kinds of policies pursued prior to the Malta summit and doing *absolutely nothing* to preserve the empire is surely much easier. *Not* providing funds to the Moscow ministries that ruined the economy in the first place, *not* dealing with as many Union institutions as possible, and *not* bestowing prizes, honors, and the like upon its statesmen are policy measures that should appeal to the inertia of government bureaucracies and that are cost-free and risk-free. It costs nothing to do nothing, and a man who has done so little to propel the Soviet Union onto the path of stable reform cannot possibly construe doing nothing as a provocation. Gorbachev will bluster, of course, and he may even make some threats, but, as should be evident by now, the USSR's last emperor, like Albert Camus's *Étranger*, can do little in the face of the benign indifference of the universe.

NOTE

I wish to thank G. P. Armstrong, Charles F. Furtado, Jr., John Halstead, Bohdan Harasymiw, Allan Kagedan, Michael Mandelbaum, and Jenik Radon for their helpful comments on earlier drafts of this essay.

4

THE SOVIET SOUTH: NATIONALISM AND THE OUTSIDE WORLD

Ronald Grigor Suny

History confounds through surprises and seemingly unpredictable events. The unfamiliar is forced upon the uninitiated, and obscure and distant places become objects of concern. What might be called the Sarajevo syndrome, an unanticipated conflict arising from ill-understood causes yet with unexpectedly far-reaching effects, was evident in February 1988 when tens of thousands of Armenians stood in the central square of Stepanakert, the district center of Nagorno-Karabakh Autonomous Oblast (NKAO) in Azerbaijan, and demanded merger with the Armenian republic. The initial demonstrations precipitated a massive response in Yerevan, the capital of Soviet Armenia, where hundreds of thousands marched through the streets; violent attacks on Armenians followed in Sumgait in neighboring Azerbaijan.

A fateful vote by the local Karabakh soviet defying official state policy and supporting the merger of Karabakh and the Armenian republic proved to be not an isolated and containable challenge, but the first sign that the fragile fabric of the Soviet Union was unraveling. The Gorbachev leadership was faced a few months later with the mobilization of the Baltic peoples, and one by one the nationalities of the USSR coalesced around separate agendas favoring a greater role for non-Russians in their own self-determination. With the emergence of the mass nationalist movements and the steady gravitation toward national political autonomy, sovereignty, and independence, the Gorbachev Revolution, largely a revolution from above, was transformed into an uncontrolled confrontation of the central state with a growing social revolution from below. A guided democratization

64

had given way to a massive anti-imperial struggle by the peoples of the Soviet Union, which has in turn delayed and distorted the center's plans for economic and political reforms and seriously limited the USSR's military and foreign policy capabilities.

Clearly, neither Sarajevo nor Karabakh and the Baltics were events without complex prior determinations. They appeared, however unexpectedly, at the conjuncture of long-term social and cultural processes with more immediate political failures. The nationalist articulation of social and political, as well as cultural, discontents was not simply a rising to the surface of a long-repressed "natural," or eternally present, national consciousness; rather, for many relatively inarticulate and inchoate ethnicities, it was the result of a long process of national formation that took place in both the centuries of tsarism and the decades of Soviet power. Unlike most of the peoples of the Soviet South, Georgians and Armenians may have had ancient kingdoms and distinct religions, languages, customs, and written traditions proclaiming their uniqueness; yet, only in the nineteenth century did nationalist intellectuals construct a coherent sense of a national past that supported political claims to autonomy or independence. Borrowed from post-1789 Europe, the ideology of political nationalism enabled ethnic intellectuals and activists to formulate their own national political visions on the basis of their particular reading of history. New "imagined communities," constructed on the basis of ethnic cultures and languages, emerged in the Caucasus and the western borderlands, but only with the greatest difficulty did the mass of peasants that made up the bulk of the ethnic communities accept their message.[1]

With the collapse of old state structures and the sundering of economic ties with the center during the years of revolution and civil war, the nationalists found an unexpected but dangerous opportunity to realize their programs. The relative weakness of the Bolsheviks before foreign interventionists briefly allowed the formation of semi-independent states in the borderlands, but by 1920–1921 the Soviets had recovered much of what they had lost (with the notable exceptions of Poland, Finland, the Baltic republics, and the western parts of Armenia,

Belorussia, and the Ukraine). When this process of nation-building started again after the revolution and civil war, it occurred within a pseudofederal Soviet state made up of ethnic territorial units and affected peoples in the east and south who had never had a national political tradition. Armenians gathered on a small part of their historic territory, which became the Armenian Soviet Socialist Republic, and began their recovery from near annihilation. Belorussians, Jews, and Ukrainians sent their children to state-sponsored schools that taught them to read in their spoken language. The Soviets divided Central Asian Muslims into new republics with no clear historic precedence and presented them with a new secular vision of nationhood. In all republics, the central government promoted political leaders from among the local people, as long as they professed loyalty to the socialist mission.

From the age of Woodrow Wilson and Vladimir Lenin on through the century, the idea that ethnicity provides legitimacy for claims to cultural and political rights and territory has had a powerful resonance, both in the USSR and throughout the world. The discourse of nationalism claims that ethnic culture and shared history give people of a particular nationality the right to control their historic territory (whether or not they make up a demographic majority) and to freely develop their culture. The Bolsheviks had incorporated this principle, axiomatic in our time, into their political program before the revolution, though the communists, once in power, often compromised or neglected entirely their own ideal of national self-determination in favor of other principles—namely, internationalism and class struggle. Yet, the form of ethnic territorial states (Union republics, autonomous republics, autonomous regions, and so forth) remained intact constitutionally, even as economic policies weakened the demographic hold of some nationalities over their territory. A fundamental tension grew between the pull toward "nativization" of ethnic territories and political structures and the pull toward acculturation and even assimilation into the larger Soviet community, the process of becoming part of a *sovetskii narod* (Soviet people). Once the limits of ethnic expression had been broadened under Gorbachev, and the legitimacy of past communist practices seriously called into question, intellectuals and activists gave voice to this tension. Fears of cultural, demographic, and linguistic degeneration combined with concern about the environment, economy, and abuses of power to create powerful nationalist movements that simultaneously represented radically democratizing impulses. Power was to devolve on the people, for they were the repository of authentic concern for the nation. Almost all major and minor nationalities in the Soviet Union, including the Great Russian, expressed a painful belief that their nations were in danger and that the communists had led them to the precipice.

Thus, paradoxically and against the expectations of the communists and most Western observers, new nations have emerged in the Soviet Union, nations stronger and more coherent than the historic ethnic communities out of which they have been constructed. From people living primarily in villages and speaking related dialects, nationalities developed that have a firmer presence in towns and cities, read and write a standardized national language, and share a sense of solidarity and common interests. We might isolate at least seven fundamental trends over the last seven decades that provide the context in which the explosion of ethnic nationalism occurred.

First, the Soviet experience, particularly in Transcaucasia and Central Asia, has included a process of nation-building, which occurred as certain ethnic and religious groups became demographically more coherent, gained new instruments and institutions with which to express and defend themselves, and began to articulate their understanding through a specifically nationalist discourse. Political nationalism had been relatively weak at the time of the Russian Revolution, concentrated largely in the urban intelligentsia, but by the 1980s nationalists had successfully elaborated a new way of looking at the world with extraordinary power to mobilize the population.

The Soviet policy of *korenizatsiia* (the promotion of national languages and national cadres in the governance of national areas), even after the Stalinist emphasis on rapid industrialization undercut it, increased the language capabilities and the politicization of the non-Russians in the national republics. The

creation of national working classes, newly urbanized populations, national intelligentsias, and ethnic political elites contributed to the more complete elaboration of nationhood.

Related to this first trend was the territorialization of ethnicity. Formerly, many ethnic and religious communities maintained their greatest loyalty to and identity with either the village
or locality in which they lived or, in the case of many Muslims, the
world Islamic community (the *umma*). Supranational and subna-
tional loyalties competed with the more specifically national.[2] For
certain ethnicities, most clearly those of Central Asia, the estab-
lishment of territorial administrative units on the basis of nationality in the early 1920s was unprecedented in their history and
provided clear political and territorial identity as alternatives to
earlier religious and tribal solidarity. Following Stalin's own defi-
nition of nation, Soviet authorities promoted an idea of nation
fixed to territory. Rather than simply identifying nationalities
with religious or ethnic culture, they linked them to special
territories, and gave privileges to titular nationalities in a kind of
affirmative action policy favoring some peoples over others.
Cosmopolitanism declined, except in parts of the Russian Soviet
Federated Socialist Republic (RSFSR), and many formerly multinational regions and cities gradually became more ethnically
homogeneous. Tbilisi, a city that Armenians and Russians had
dominated both demographically and politically before the Revolution, first achieved a Georgian majority in the 1960s. Baku
steadily became Azerbaijani in the Soviet period; ultimately, in a
paroxysm of national fervor, Azerbaijanis finally drove the large
Armenian minority, along with many Russians and Jews, from
the city in January 1990. Yerevan, which as a small town in the
late nineteenth century still contained a large Muslim population, grew into a nearly purely Armenian city through the in-
migration of Armenians from other parts of the Soviet Union
and the Armenian diaspora.

Third, relations between the center and the ethnic periph-
eries were basically imperial, that is, inequitable and based on a
subordinate relationship to the Russian center. As Russian was
closely identified with Soviet, with proletarian, and with progress
(and all the incumbent privileges), ethnicity determined a cer-

tain degree of advantage and disadvantage. In many ways, from the early 1930s, ethnicity became far more important than class as a marker in Soviet society of social position, access to power and information, mobility, and so forth. By 1974, the government had eliminated class designations, so key to social promotion in the early Soviet period, from the internal passport that Soviet citizens were required to carry. But ethnicity remained as a fundamental determinant of official identity, which at one and the same time made people eligible for promotion and access to privileges (if, for example, they were members of the titular nationality of a given republic) and for discrimination (if they were not).

While native cadres may have governed in Azerbaijan or Uzbekistan (particularly after the 1920s, when native communists were few), Moscow largely determined policies, and local interests were subordinated to all-Union goals. The government treated non-Russian republics as objects of central policy rather than subjects capable of independent decision making, thereby fundamentally altering their national destiny. In Kazakhstan, for example, the imposition of collectivization of agriculture resulted in the loss of 40 percent of the population through either death or migration. Moscow forcibly settled a nomadic population on the land, fundamentally changing its ancient way of life. Industrial and agricultural development, particularly Khrushchev's Virgin Lands program of the 1950s, resulted in the settlement of non-Kazakhs in the republic, and by 1979 Kazakhs made up only 33 percent of the area's population. Moreover, Kazakhstan became a test area for atomic weapons and proving ground for up-and-coming party leaders like Leonid Brezhnev, who served as party chief in 1955–1956.[3]

Fourth, even as Moscow was strengthening ethnicity in many ways, it was limiting and even undermining it in others. Official Soviet policy spoke for years of *sblizhenie* (rapprochement) and *sliianie* (merger) of Soviet peoples and of the creation of a single Soviet culture. Mobility, acculturation of political and intellectual elites, the preference for Russian schooling, and the generalized effects of modernization all created anxiety about assimilation and loss of culture. A deep contradiction developed during the Soviet years between the pressures resulting from modernization and state policies promoting assimilation, on the one hand, and the effects of *korenizatsiia* and the "renationaliza-tion" of ethnic groups, on the other. Stronger, more coherent, and more ethnically conscious nations faced an uncertain future in a political system in which they had little say over their fate.

The contradictory Soviet policies, combined with different historic levels of development and proximity to the dominant nation, had wide-ranging effects among various peoples. Some nationalities suffered extraordinarily from Russification, nota-bly the Belorussians (no Belorussian schools were available in the republic's cities); others, like the Armenians and Georgians, felt little effect, though they often complained bitterly about the impositions of a bilingualist policy. The in-migration of Russians and other Slavs weakened several nationalities—notably the Ka-zakhs, Estonians, and Latvians—though other nationalities—the Armenians, Azerbaijanis, and Georgians, for example—in-creased their percentages in the republics' population. Estonians and Georgians vigorously resisted learning Russian and de-fended native language use, while hundreds of thousands of Ukrainians lost the ability to communicate with ease in the lan-guage of their grandparents.

Fifth, for all the transformative effects of Soviet-style mod-ernization, traditional cultures have persisted. What Gregory Massell calls "the old unities based on kinship, custom, and belief" have managed to survive even as Moscow has removed traditional leaderships, officially undermined religion, and fun-damentally changed the social environment.[4] In Central Asia, the lack of a native proletariat and clearly delineated class lines led the regime in the 1920s to attempt to use women as a "surro-gate proletariat," an improvised "class" wedge to force cleavages in traditional Muslim societies. The leadership encouraged women to take off their veils, seek work outside the household, and challenge the patriarchal authority of their fathers and brothers. The experiment, which was extremely costly in human life, especially among communist cadres and their supporters, was, at least in the short run, a failure, as women who had given up the veil returned to the ancient practice. "For the most part, women may be said to have failed to function as a social class, a stratum with a sense of shared identity, with a distinct, clearly perceived community of experience, interest, purpose, and action."[5]

The local, traditional sociocultural systems of the prerevolutionary period, segmented and small in scale, were resistant to forced change from outside and provided places of retreat from Soviet interventions. In Georgia, for example, "the sense of powerlessness of villagers towards the state encourages them to turn inwards."[6] Kinship networks and the mistrust of outsiders combine to encourage the use of unofficial, informal means of settling conflicts. Socialization still takes place in the family, and women, as the guardians of the Georgian tradition, teach their children both the values of the culture and a wariness toward the larger Soviet world.[7] Patronage networks, so central in Transcaucasia to an individual's power and prestige, are carefully maintained and have been adapted to the requirements of an economy of shortages.[8]

Sixth, the very nature of Soviet modernization created sharp divisions not only between nationalities but also within nationalities. Soviet economic and social change has been extremely uneven, and the result has been the coexistence of mobile, better-educated, more modern urban populations with less mobile, less educated, traditional societies in the countryside. A lack of resources is partly responsible, making the full transformation of all parts of Soviet society economically too costly, but Soviet policies also have been a factor, whether consciously or unconsciously. Faced with a choice between only implementing large-scale economic change and simultaneously carrying out a cultural revolution, the Stalinist regime retreated from the more radical cultural practices of the 1920s and tolerated "distinctly uneven development in political, economic, and socio-cultural spheres—indeed [displayed] a willingness to leave pockets of antecedent life-styles relatively undisturbed, if necessary, for an indefinite period of time."[9] In her ethnography of a Georgian village, Tamara Dragadze demonstrates that even collectivization did little to change traditional settlement patterns or redistribute wealth in the villages of Ratcha. Soviet practices actually fostered rather than undercut family solidarity. "Soviet law re-enforces the age-old tradition whereby a son lives next to his parents, with nearby houses belonging to his brothers, paternal uncles and first cousins. . . . Throughout the country, the family provides more support and demands greater loyalty than any other institution. The government has refrained from inter-fering in this, except for campaigning against nepotism and overspending at family celebrations."[10]

Seventh, the political leadership of the Communist Party, even as it proclaimed the full resolution of the "national ques-tion" in the Soviet Union, failed to deal effectively with the problems of a multinational empire and in turn created new problems. Bolshevism had long reduced problems of nationality and ethnic culture to economics, failing to appreciate the inde-pendent power of ethnic culture. Though granting that nation-ality had to be accommodated before the full victory of communism, Bolshevism was consistently suspicious of national expression. Over time, and even at a given moment, Bolshevik policy was profoundly inconsistent, on the one hand pushing for nativization and the flourishing (*rastsvet*) of national cultures, while on the other promoting the ideological goals of *stiranie* (obliteration of national peculiarities), *sblizhenie,* and *sliianie.* The regime retained full power to decide what was permissible "pa-triotic" expression and what was pernicious nationalism, and the boundaries between the two shifted constantly.[11]

In the Khrushchev and Brezhnev years, the arena of allow-able national expression expanded considerably, and republican leaderships forged their own ties between their populations through the manipulation of ethnic symbols. At the same time, the loosening of control from the center after Stalin's death permitted regional and ethnic communist parties to operate increasingly independently of Moscow. The rise of ethnic "mafias" centered in national communist parties fostered cor-ruption and threatened the overall development of the Soviet economy. The regime itself had become an obstacle to the growth both of the economy and of society.

One can argue that nationalism has been a growing pres-ence in all parts of the world in our century, and that the very processes of urbanization and industrialization, the spread of mass education, and greater access to print and other media aid the consolidation of ethnolinguistic groups; nevertheless, nation-building in the USSR has created a particularly volatile set of problems. A number of conscious, secular, politically mobilized nationalities now exist where they had not previously existed, and with their greater coherence and consciousness, nationalist leaders have been able to command mass followings that had earlier eluded them. Rather than undermining nationalism, the processes of industrialization, urbanization, and state-building in the Soviet Union have provided the social and cultural base for a fierce nationalist opposition to Communist Party rule. When the top party leadership decided to radically reform the political system, it, at one and the same time, began a process of delegitimizing the Soviet system and giving political voice to the nationalist alternative.

CURRENT COMPLEXITIES AND GORBACHEV'S DILEMMAS

When Gorbachev came to power in March 1985, the Soviet state was already in a profoundly weakened condition. The USSR had experienced not only years of political and economic stagnation, but a frustrating absence of able and stable leadership in the first half of the 1980s. Weakness in the center had enabled the local ethnic and regional mafias within the party-state apparatus to increase their power. Moreover, the USSR was internationally isolated, bogged down in a draining war in Afghanistan, and facing an aggressively hostile American president. To restart the Soviet economic engine and restore the country's position internationally, Gorbachev needed first to build a political base for his program of reform, not least of all in the non-Russian republics. "Probably the most concentrated opposition to Gorbachev's leadership and his policies," writes Martha Brill Olcott, "has come from the party and state bureaucracies in the national republics."[12]

Gorbachev was caught between, on the one hand, nationality leaderships that opposed his reforms, and, on the other, intellectual and popular forces, most of which, once they overcame their suspicion of the Kremlin, were interested in the general liberalizing thrust of Moscow's new policies. In Transcaucasia and Central Asia, a series of purges (1985–1988) eliminated the top leaders in nearly every republic, not always without resistance. In Kazakhstan, the removal of longtime party chief Dinmukhamed Kunaev and his replacement by a Russian, Gennadii Kolbin, brought demonstrators into the streets in December 1986. Prolonged pressure from the center on the Armenian party did not achieve the desired removal of Karen Demirchian from the post of first secretary until the Karabakh crisis exploded and Moscow could more directly intervene. But these interventions hardly touched the political control over the southern republics by locally based mafias. When the "democratic" forces began to act, as with the Karabakh movement, the emergence of mass nationalist popular fronts burst asunder the very bounds of the old politics and rapidly undermined the power of local communist parties, even those whose leaderships Moscow had renewed. With the general democratization of political practices, the delegitimization of Communist Party rule in general, and the growing reluctance and inefficacy of the center to use force to impose its will (the Tbilisi syndrome), nationalist movements gradually pushed the old political classes from power.

Since 1989, nationalists and their allies have been attempting to constitute themselves as a new political class, more successfully in some republics than in others. In Armenia, the Pan-Armenian National Movement (HHSh) took hold of the reins of government in August 1990, successfully negotiated with President Gorbachev to bring order to the republic, and declared Armenia sovereign and independent. In Azerbaijan, which has been under "Soviet occupation" since January 1990, the Communist Party, propped up by the Soviet army, has reasserted itself and displaced the Azerbaijani Popular Front. The two principal political forces eye each other suspiciously, and each promotes itself as the legitimate representative of Azerbaijani nationhood. In Georgia, the religious nationalists around Zviad Gamsakhurdia won the November 1990 elections and aim to lead the country to full independence, but the political movement remains extraordinarily fissiparous. In Central Asia, the old communist parties still have considerable power, particularly in Turkmenistan, and have appropriated much of the program of the national fronts.

With the growing weakness of the center and the new independence of the republics (and of ethnic minorities within republics), Gorbachev is faced with an irresolvable dilemma, "a cruel choice"—as Paul Goble succinctly puts it—"whether to pursue his democratization programs at the expense of control over the periphery or to maintain control at the cost of his broader policy agenda."[13] And all this against the background of an accelerating economic meltdown.

Allied to this dilemma is the conflict between the leadership of the Soviet army, which wants to preserve the army as a disciplined multinational instrument of state policy, and the popular and ethnic aspirations for a decentralized, nationalized military force that could not be used to repress national movements. At the September 1989 Central Committee plenum on nationalities, Defense Minister Dmitrii Yazov strongly condemned "certain negative phenomena that have arisen in a number of republics [that] have begun to penetrate into soldiers' barracks and sailors' quarters," and complained that "the label of 'occupying forces' is pinned on Soviet fighting men." He expressed horror at the "increasingly open calls to split our Army into national segments" and called for "effective concern for the study of the Russian language in the Union republics. . . . Last year, however, the number of inductees with practically no command of the Russian language exceeded 125,000. This is 12 times more than 20 years ago. An alarming trend."[14]

Not only do Transcaucasians and Central Asians want military units in their republics to be under local authority, not only do they not want their young men and women to serve outside the republic, but Russians, as in the Stavropol demonstrations in January 1990, have begun to resist sending their sons and daughters to settle ethnic conflicts in other republics. Central Asians and Transcaucasians believe that they are especially discriminated against within the armed forces, the frequent victims of condescension and harassment (*dedovshchina*) from officers and fellow soldiers.[15] In Armenia and Azerbaijan, popular militias have formed to defend the republics (or particular political interests) in what they consider the absence of sufficient protection from Soviet forces.[16] The army itself has signaled its unhappiness with being used as a police force to settle internal social and ethnic conflicts.

Faced by stronger, more coherent non-Russian nations than have ever existed in the Soviet period—or, indeed, than existed in the tsarist period—Gorbachev has been unable to find a political language powerful enough to substitute for the various nationalist discourses. His last-ditch argument has been (as early in 1990, during the crisis over Lithuanian independence) that nationalism, republican sovereignty, or secession would most extremely undermine the reform movement and the president himself. As the reality of republican independence grows day by day, as Moscow proves incapable of reestablishing its authority, the various nationalisms have become the only effective ideological and political choice for the Soviet peoples. At issue is no longer where they came from or how they grew so powerful, but how they shall be dealt with in a partnership of equality and respect. For the foreseeable future, nationalism will be the dominant discourse for non-Russians and for a significant number of Russians, as well. Communists will either accommodate themselves to it, as Boris Yeltsin has been trying to do, or be out of the game.

In the summer and fall of 1990, one ever more frequently heard people talk either of proceeding boldly along the democratic path, even if this meant the breakup of the Soviet Union, or of retreating to a more authoritarian alternative, the forceful preservation of the Union by a military takeover. The physical and moral forces were simply not there for a compelled return to anything resembling Brezhnev's stable, stagnant Soviet Union. Gorbachev accomplished his enormous success in dismantling the Communist Party's monopoly on power by maintaining a broad political coalition, taking hesitant steps toward democracy, and making tactical retreats to prevent reaction from the conservatives in the apparatus. But by mid-1990, critics cited his policies of compromise and half-measures as the cause for the political and economic breakdown. As the year came to an end, the Soviet president undertook stronger measures to relieve the food shortages, placate the restive army leaders, and push through his version of a new Union treaty with the republics. And in January 1991, tanks rolled into Lithuania in an attempt to force the local leaders to give up their drive for independence.

After decades of neglecting the non-Russian peoples of the USSR and treating the Soviet Union as if it were little more than an ethnically Russian state, Western sovietologists and journalists now show signs of another form of myopia by not looking more critically at the current nationalism. Many Western social scientists, journalists, and pundits, following the lead of the nationalists themselves, argue that ethnic ties are so powerful that other claims to identity and cohesion, such as class, gender, or generation, need not be taken seriously. Yet some students of individual nationalist movements have noted the fracturing of those movements and the reproduction of divisions within ethnic societies that make it problematic to speak of "the Georgians" or "the Uzbeks." Class, gender, regional, urban-rural, and generational differences are asserting themselves and being newly articulated as challenges to the more inclusive nationalist discourses within the republics.

Moreover, the intensity of nationalism at a given moment is contingent on specific economic, social, and political conjunctures. Though nationalism is not reducible to economics, the relationship between economic hardships and inequities, on the one hand, and ethnic hostilities, on the other, has been brutally demonstrated in Karabakh, the Ferghana Valley, Moldova, and elsewhere. The chronic economic crisis in the USSR has helped to erode support for the Soviet system, for socialism, and for Communist Party rule; it has also buttressed nationalist arguments that the non-Russian republics can do better on their own. Independence seems to be the answer both to cultural grievances and to more mundane material problems of everyday life. Yet, with independence from the USSR, the old enemy will be eliminated, and social and cultural cleavages within each nationality will become more visible.

Already in some republics it is clear that the moment of the nationalist intelligentsia, those brave former dissidents or newly coined patriots who first manned the barricades, may be coming to an end as other social groups, some far less educated and urbanized, arise to take over these movements. In Azerbaijan, for example, the initial founders of the Popular Front lost out by the end of 1989 to others who spoke a more militant language of hostility, not only toward Armenians, but also against people of privilege—intellectuals, Baku city dwellers, the apparatus—all of whom were linked in some nefarious ways. The intellectuals later excused themselves from any responsibility in the massacres in Baku by blaming them on those who had displaced them and on emigrants from Armenia.[17]

In Armenia, the intelligentsia appears to be victorious at the moment, having successfully disarmed the paramilitary opponents of the HHSh, but it is far from united. In Georgia, the nationalists suffer from an even more extreme fractiousness (reportedly, over 100 political parties exist there). Two major coalitions—the Roundtable of Gamsakhurdia and the National Congress led by Giorgi Chanturia—circle each other like tired wrestlers. In Central Asia, where distinct intellectual elites separate from or in opposition to the older political establishments had not long existed, informal groups and popular fronts appeared later than in the Caucasus and the Baltic.[18] Despite being discredited through the public exposure of corruption, most dramatically in Uzbekistan, where it was linked to the Brezhnev family, the old apparatus remains firmly in power in most of the republics of the region.

INTERETHNIC CONFLICTS AND DIASPORAS

Within each Soviet republic live ethnic minorities that have been putting forth cultural and political demands. In Transcaucasia, the most volatile conflicts have been between the Armenians living in NKAO and the Azerbaijanis, who dominate the republic. Armenians make up the overwhelming majority of the population of NKAO and desire merger with the neighboring Armenian republic. Azerbaijanis represent about a quarter of the population of the region and hold that Karabakh is part of their national patrimony. As a result of the fierce fighting around this issue, hundreds of thousands of Azerbaijanis have fled from the Armenian republic. Armenians in Azerbaijan began to emigrate after the February 1988 killings of Armenians in Sumgait, but their final removal occurred in January 1990, when mobs turned on the Armenians of Baku.

The growing power of the nationalists frightened the Abkhazian minority in the western part of Georgia and the Osetins in the northeast. Abkhazians, numbering fewer than 100,000, make up only 17 percent of the Abkhaz autonomous republic's population, but they had been accorded cultural and political privileges in the last few decades. Georgians, who make up the largest ethnicity in the autonomous republic (44 percent), resented the advantages that Abkhazians enjoyed, and some of the more extreme nationalists called for the abolition of Abkhaz autonomy. Similar conflicts arose in South Osetia, where the Osetins make up 66 percent of the autonomous region. In 1989, the Osetins unilaterally raised the status of their region to autonomous republic, and in September 1990, they declared the South Osetin Soviet Democratic Republic to be independent of Georgia and a part of the USSR.

Almost all the major and many of the minor nationalities of the Soviet South have diaspora populations both within and outside the USSR. The borders of the national states in the Soviet Union, particularly in Central Asia, did not (and could not) coincide with the mixed ethnic populations of the region. Large numbers of Uzbeks were left in Kirghizia, Tajiks in Uzbekistan (particularly in cities), and so on. Of the 6 million Volga or Kazan Tatars in the Soviet Union, only 1.8 million live in the Tatar republic. In Georgia, Armenians live compactly in Akhaltsikhe and Akhalkalaki, and are more dispersed in Tbilisi and Abkhazia. A large Armenian community of well-educated and well-placed professionals lived in Baku until 1990, not to mention that 75 percent of the population of NKAO was (and probably still is) Armenian. Georgians, known as Ingilos, live in Azerbaijan, and hundreds of thousands of Azerbaijanis live in Georgia and lived in Armenia until the Karabakh conflict made their situation precarious. Each of these populations has experienced either conflict and violence or a rising sense of insecurity and vulnerability.

The killings of Meskhetian Turks by Uzbeks in the Ferghana Valley (June 1989), and the violence in Novyi Uzhen (Uzbekistan) directed at Lezgins from the North Caucasus (June 1989), along the Tajik-Kirghiz border (late summer 1989), and in Osh between Kirghiz and Uzbeks (June 1990) brutally blurred the vision of Muslim unity among the 50-odd million Soviet Muslims. In each of these cases, as well as in the instances of attacks on Armenians and other "outsiders," the context of violence appears to be high levels of unemployment, lack of decent housing, and pressure on the land. In a world in which ethnicity defines privilege and access, economic discontents crystallize around ethnic divisions.

One of the fault lines dividing Soviet Muslims, for example, cuts the Turkic-speaking peoples off from the Iranian-speaking Tajiks. Tajikistan, which was carved out of part of the former Bukharan khanate (later Bukharan People's Soviet Republic) in 1924 (the rest going to the new Uzbek Soviet Socialist Republic), is 62 percent Tajik, 23.5 percent Uzbek, and 7.6 percent Russian. One-quarter of all Soviet Tajiks live outside the republic, with nearly a million Tajiks living in Uzbekistan (4.7 percent of the population) alone. Relations between Tajiks and Uzbeks have never been without tension. Tajiks make up a large part of the urban population of Samarkand and Bukhara and pride themselves on their intellectual traditions, which go back to pre-Soviet times, when Persian was the principal language of intellectual and religious exchange in Central Asia. Younger Tajiks in particular are more resistant to Turkic culture and demonstrate interest in closer cultural ties with Iran. Particularly grating is the absence of adequate Tajik educational institutions in Uzbekistan while Uzbeks in Tajikistan have their own schools.[19] When ethnic violence broke out in Tajikistan in February 1990, however, the crowds turned on Armenians, whom they thought were being settled in Dushambe after the pogroms in Baku. Here, economic and social problems—shortages of apartments, preferences ostensibly given to outsiders—provided the tinder for an explosion displaced onto ethnic grounds.

While the Armenian diaspora is the most far-flung, ranging from neighboring Iran and Turkey (largely in Istanbul) to Los Angeles and Fresno, the Azerbaijanis have the distinction that the great majority of their ethnic community resides across the Arax River in Iran (in 1989, some 6.8 million Azerbaijanis lived in Soviet Azerbaijan, roughly 8 million in Iran, and another 400,000 in Turkey). Georgians have a small community of compatriots near the Black Sea in Turkey, and most of the Central Asian peoples have large numbers of conationals living across the border (see Table 2 in Appendix I).

The most dramatic attempt to link up with compatriots on the other side of the border occurred at the very end of 1989, when Soviet Azerbaijanis in Nakhichevan tore down border posts and fences and spontaneously opened up the border. After some initial attempts to restore the old order, Soviet troops did not intervene until the January invasion of the republic. The initiative for reestablishing ties with southern Azerbaijan (northern Iran), which had been separated from the north since the 1820s, came almost completely from the Soviet side. The Soviet Azerbaijani intelligentsia had long harbored desires, reflected in the so-called literature of longing, for unity with southern Azerbaijan, and leading writers had been involved in the short-lived attempt to establish an independent republic in the region after World War II.[20]

But the Iranian side has not shared Soviet Azerbaijanis' enthusiasm for unity. Ali Akbar Rafsanjani, the president of Iran, visited Baku in June 1989, and Sheikh ul-Isam Allkhshukur Pashazade, the spiritual leader of Soviet Shiite Muslims, traveled to Iran, where he concluded an agreement with Iranian clerics to train Soviet religious students in Iranian madrassahs; nevertheless, the Iranian government remained wary of upsetting the fragile relations with the Soviet Union, particularly at a time of international isolation. Preventing the formation of a unified Azerbaijan must be a concern for the Iranian government, and is analogous to Iran's opposition to the creation of a Kurdish national state. Azerbaijani intellectuals from Baku have expressed much more interest in ties with Turkey, whose people are their linguistic brethren, than with Iran, with whose population they share the Shiite faith. While Islamic symbols, green flags, even portraits of Khomeini, certainly have appeared in the streets of Baku, the movement in Azerbaijan has had a predominantly nationalist, rather than Islamic, character, focusing most powerfully on a sense of Azerbaijan as an ethnic territorial nation.[21] Islam and nation pull in different directions—one toward the universal Muslim community (the *umma*), the other toward a specific territory defined by ethnicity. At times they can also be melded into a single nationalism, as in Iran, Iraq, and elsewhere. But here, rather than Islam's having been the impulse behind Azerbaijani nationalism, the "Armenian threat" in the context of economic decline, unemployment, popular political impotence, and a discredited ruling elite brought the crowds out to defend the territorial integrity of Azerbaijan. The rhetoric directed against the Armenian claims to Karabakh has been about the dismembering of the homeland, and Azerbaijanis now see Karabakh as the heartland of Azerbaijan.

The disintegration of the Soviet Union presents Iran with more dangers than opportunities. Internally, the latter must continue to manage resident Azerbaijanis, who for decades under the Pahlavis and more recently under the mullahs have not been permitted to have their own schools. Though this has apparently retarded the development and spread of the kinds of ethnic nationalist or Pan-Turkic consciousness the population in the north has experienced, the potential to become a self-conscious and mobilized nationality could suddenly be actualized.[22] As the largest minority in Iran, the Azerbaijanis are a relatively well-integrated, relatively prosperous part of Iranian society. Up to now, they have understood that theocratic Iran deals firmly with any separatist ambitions, or even mild dissension, like that of the Azerbaijani Ayatollah Kazim Shariat Madari, who was confined to house arrest after Khomeini came to power.

The Armenian-Azerbaijani conflict has resonated in the Turkish press and political circles. The harshest voices against Armenians and in favor of their "Turkic brothers" in Azerbaijan have come from the political and clerical right, for example, the newspaper *Terjuman.* Shortly after the invasion of Azerbaijan, *The New York Times* reported pro-Azerbaijani demonstrations, calling for tougher attitudes toward the Soviet Union, in the Turkish town of Igdir, near the Armenian border, as well as in Istanbul and Ankara.[23] Once the shock over "Black January" subsided, cooler voices could also be heard. In September, a reporter from *Milliyet,* who had been graciously received in Armenia, wrote a series of articles advocating better relations with the Armenians. While many Armenians in the diaspora fear that an independent Armenia, set adrift by the Russians, will fall victim to Azerbaijani aggression or to a new Turkish dream of Pan-Turkic unification, the Turkish government's sights seem to be set on Europe, not on Yerevan. While no influential Turkish politician is willing to suggest that Turkey ought to acknowledge the Ottoman genocide of the Armenians in 1915, many are aware that an attack on Armenia would only confirm the image of the "Terrible Turk," so fixed in the European mind. Ever since the early postwar crises that froze the lines of the Cold War alliances, Turkey, like Iran, has learned to live with its Soviet neighbor in relative tranquillity. The current situation is fraught with uncertainty and may threaten Turkey's campaign for membership in the European Community.

THE VIEW FROM WASHINGTON

Americans might grow nostalgic in the coming years for the old Soviet Union and its policies, which in a general way were at least consistent and predictable. For 45 years, the Soviet Union had not moved its troops beyond its positions in 1945, with the single exception of the intervention into Afghanistan in 1979. For nearly half a century, the countries of Eastern Europe could be discounted as independent actors—again with notable exceptions, like Ceaucescu's Romania—and subsumed under an integrated policy toward the Soviet bloc. The situation clearly is much more complicated today, as more and more new players enter the international arena. The goals of American policy during the Cold War, from rollback to polycentrism in Eastern

Europe, appear to have been realized, though hardly in any imaginable scenario of those years.

With multiple centers of decision making emerging in Eastern Europe and the Soviet Union, some analysts have warned that bold moves by the United States at this time would be counterproductive. Americans might profitably, cautiously, "simply sit on their hands and watch while the drama unfolds."[24] The Soviet Union, after all, will for some time be a weaker state than it has been since the Cold War, and one may argue that the chaos in and collapse of the Soviet empire serve American interests well. In any case, it is doubtful whether any American initiative would have much effect on the processes of radical disintegration now taking place within what is left of the USSR.

It might appear that this passive approach would minimize risks for the United States; if one accepts, however, that long-term chaos, instability, and unpredictability would not be in America's interest, then disintegration of the Soviet Union may be undesirable from Washington's point of view. Since reconstruction of the old empire is no longer possible without an abrupt turn away from glasnost and *demokratizatsiia,* the United States might do best to devise a policy that would encourage continued openness and democratization but also preserve some, however minimal, central state authority. In place of the Soviet federation, the United States might use its influence in whatever ways possible to promote a loose confederation of sovereign republics, tied together in a voluntary agreement, that would at least provide a central authority responsible for defense (and nuclear weapons), be available as a third-party mediator between rival republics, and act as arbitrator in interethnic conflicts between dominant nationalities and minorities within republics.

Regrettably, many of the republics, including the RSFSR, are rejecting such a proposal, put forth by President Gorbachev. Day by day, this solution appears less viable as the economic collapse loosens the fragile ties between the republics and the center. Yet, the alternative to some kind of confederation may be prolonged civil and ethnic wars. The United States could provide aid and support, much of it at a substate level, to bolster the failing economy and the Gorbachev presidency. An agency for developing democracy and enterprise in the former Soviet Union, sponsored and funded by the U.S. government, could manage aid programs of a nonmilitary nature. Given that 70 years of Soviet socialism has engendered support for welfarist and protectionist state programs among the Soviet people, this agency should be prepared to encourage not only private enterprise, but a range of collective, cooperative, joint state-private, and state enterprises. It might stress aid in noncontroversial areas that are popular with the nationalist movements and override particular ethnic interests, such as ecology. Sociologist and People's Deputy to the USSR Congress Liudmilla Harutiunian has advocated "incentives for those wishing to remain faithful to the existing ties of cooperation." As an example, she mentioned that the cleanup of Chernobyl and its effects should be declared an all-Union responsibility, for it is far beyond the resources of, for example, Belorussia.[25] This would support both the market economy and the Gorbachev presidency.

The United States has unique resources to exploit in its engagement with post-Soviet society. Besides possessing enormous wealth and developed technology, and offering an example of electoral politics, the United States is home to diaspora populations from the USSR, notably Armenians, Baltic peoples, Jews, and Ukrainians. Many of these peoples are interested in helping their compatriots in the homeland; some, like the Armenian relief organizations set up to aid Armenia after the earthquake of December 1988, are already deeply involved in helping their conationals. Diasporas can be mobilized and funded to develop monitored projects, for both economic development and democratic political evolution.

The United States can ill afford to either allow the complete disintegration of the Soviet Union, which has already been characterized as Lebanonization, or wait until a new, brutal central authority, whether military or Russian imperialist or fascist, recreates by force a post-Soviet empire. Its interests in economic development as a prerequisite for stability and further democratic political development can best be realized if some central authority, however weak compared with the old Soviet state, is preserved. In many ways, the post-Soviet confederation could resemble the West European economic and political union. Both would be loose, yet integrated, economic blocs made up of sovereign states. Exactly what prerogatives would be surrendered to the center will be the subject of negotiations in both parts of Europe for many years, or perhaps decades, to come.

A large, more democratic, multinational state or integrated system of states will present a unique set of problems and opportunities for the United States, just as the greater economic and political unity of Western Europe will. The creation of the European Community and the end of the Cold War will inevitably transform the American military and economic role in Europe. The end of communism as we have known it also means the end of anticommunism as we have known it. One might reasonably hope that Gorbachev's example of revolutionizing international relations through "new thinking" will prove contagious.

NOTES

1. For this view, I am indebted to Benedict Anderson, *Imagined Communities: Reflections on the Origin and Spread of Nationalism* (London: Verso, 1983). On the "constructedness" of nationality, see also Ernest Gellner, *Thought and Change* (London: Weidenfeld and Nicolson, 1964); Tom Nairn, *The Break-up of Britain* (London: New Left Books, 1977); and Geoff Eley, "Nationalism and Social History," *Social History* 6, no. 1 (January 1981), pp. 83–107.

2. Alexandre Bennigsen, "Several Nations or One People," *Survey,* no. 108 (1979), pp. 51 ff.; Michael Rywkin, *Moscow's Muslim Challenge: Soviet Central Asia* (Armonk, N.Y.: M. E. Sharpe, 1982), p. 118. Bennigsen concluded, I believe wrongly, that for Soviet Muslims, the national—the allegiance to the national Soviet republics—was the weakest loyalty, while the supranational—allegiance to the Islamic community of Central Asia as a whole—was the strongest.

3. On Kazakhstan, see Martha Brill Olcott, *The Kazakhs* (Stanford, Calif.: Hoover Institution Press, 1987).

4. Gregory J. Massell, *The Surrogate Proletariat: Moslem Women and Revolutionary Strategies in Soviet Central Asia, 1919–1929* (Princeton, N.J.: Princeton University Press, 1974), p. 83.

5. Ibid., p. 397.

6. Tamara Dragadze, *Rural Families in Soviet Georgia: A Case Study in Ratcha Province* (London and New York: Routledge, 1988), p. 199.

7. Ibid., pp. 137–138.

8. Gerald Mars and Yochanan Altman, "The Cultural Bases of Soviet Georgia's Second Economy," *Soviet Studies* 35, no. 4 (October 1983), pp. 546–560.

9. Massell, *The Surrogate Proletariat,* p. 409.

10. Tamara Dragadze, "Family Life in Georgia," *New Society,* August 19, 1976.

11. Massell, *The Surrogate Proletariat,* p. 60.

12. Martha Brill Olcott, "Gorbachev's Nationalities Policy and Central Asia," in Rajan Menon and Daniel N. Nelson, eds., *Limits to Soviet Power* (Lexington, Mass.: Lexington Books, 1989), pp. 69–70.

13. Paul Goble, "Moscow's Nationality Problems in 1989," *Report on the USSR* 2, no. 2 (January 12, 1990), p. 13.

14. *Pravda,* September 22, 1989; *Current Digest of the Soviet Press* 61, no. 40 (November 1, 1989), p. 17; and Stephen Foye, "Defense Minister Yazov: Friend or Foe of Military Reforms?" *Report on the USSR* 1, no. 44 (November 3, 1989), pp. 16–17.

15. James Critchlow, "Uzbek Army Recruits Believed Murdered to Avenge Ferghana Killings," *Report on the USSR* 1, no. 44 (November 3, 1989), pp. 23–25.

16. In August and September 1990, these paramilitary units were either disarmed or integrated into the state forces under the general supervision of the newly elected noncommunist Armenian government.

17. In most accounts, the perpetrators of the killings are said to be Azerbaijani emigrants from Armenia. See Elizabeth Fuller, "Gorbachev's Dilemma in Azerbaijan," *Report on the USSR* 2, no. 5 (February 2, 1990), pp. 14–16. Fuller writes: "(Vezirov disclosed not long ago that up to half a million Azerbaijanis are unemployed. In Baku—a city of 1.7 million—68,000 families do not have proper accommodation, and 200,000 people live in shanty towns [*samostroiki*].) It is this dispossessed underclass that was among the main perpetrators of the anti-Armenian pogroms earlier this month, according to world chess champion Gary Kasparov, himself a native of Baku" (p. 15). Bill Keller picked up this view of some Azerbaijani intellectuals in his remarkable (and disturbing) piece, "Did Moscow Incite Azerbaijanis? Some See a Plot," *New York Times,* February 19, 1990, p. A6; Keller also reports rumors of Kremlin provocation.

18. Bess Brown, "The Role of Public Groups in *Perestroika* in Central Asia," *Report on the USSR* 2, no. 4 (January 26, 1990), pp. 20–25.

19. Eden Naby, "Tajiks Reemphasize Iranian Heritage as Ethnic Pressures Mount in Central Asia," *Report on the USSR* 2, no. 7 (February 16, 1990), pp. 20–22; and the following articles in *Report on the USSR* 2, no. 8 (February 23, 1990)—James Critchlow, "Tajik Scholar Describes a Source of Ethnic Discontent," pp. 19–20; Suzanne Crow, "Informal Groups in Tajikistan—Will They Have a Role?" pp. 20–21; and Bess Brown, "Unrest in Tajikistan," pp. 28–31.

20. David B. Nissman, *The Soviet Union and Iranian Azerbaijan: The Use of Nationalism for Political Penetration* (Boulder, Colo., and London: Westview Press, 1987).

21. Anthony Hyman, "Soviet-Iranian Relations: The End of Rapprochement?" *Report on the USSR* 2, no. 4 (January 26, 1990), pp. 17–18.

22. For a reading that emphasizes the growing Pan-Turkic feelings in Tabriz, see Anthony Hyman, "Soviet-Iranian Relations and the Two Azerbaijans," *Report on the USSR* 2, no. 2 (January 12, 1990), pp. 15–16.
23. Alan Cowell, "Turks at Rally Assail Soviet Moves," *The New York Times*, January 26, 1990, p. A7.
24. Olcott, "Gorbachev's Nationalities Policy and Central Asia," pp. 87–88.
25. "Union Treaty Through the Labyrinth," *Moscow News*, November 25–December 2, 1990, pp. 8–9.

5

THE SOVIET "NATIONALITY FRONT": SOME IMPLICATIONS FOR U.S. FOREIGN AND SECURITY POLICY

Jeremy R. Azrael

Until recently, U.S. policymakers and policy planners took it for granted that the Soviet Union would enter the 21st century as a unified country. The Baltic states might eventually gain their political independence, but the rest of the Soviet Union, it was assumed, would stay intact. The great uncertainty was not *whether* the USSR, but *whither*. Would Gorbachev and his colleagues succeed in transforming the Soviet Union into a "normal" country—that is, a country with a functioning economy, a civil society, a democratic regime, and a "civilized" foreign policy? Or would conservative opposition, bureaucratic resistance, and social inertia prove impossible to overcome? In the former case, U.S.–Soviet relations would cease to be essentially adversarial and might even become extremely close. In the latter, the Soviet challenge to U.S. interests would persist, albeit in somewhat less militant and less intimidating form.

As a result of fast-paced developments on the "nationality front," the realization is growing in Washington, as elsewhere, that this presumed alternative has been overtaken by events. Instead of normalizing or backsliding, the Soviet Union seems to be disintegrating before our very eyes. Rising national self-consciousness and self-assertiveness have completely shattered the myth that the peoples of the Soviet Union have drawn significantly closer during the past 70 years, let alone merged—to use the Soviet term—into a single, supranational Soviet people. In many cases, in fact, it seems clear that Sovietization actually impeded what might otherwise have been a more or less rapid process of ethnopolitical integration. In any event, an upsurge of grass-roots nationalism has combined with a rapid breakdown of the governmental infrastructure to create a situation that invites comparison with nothing so much as the Ottoman empire on the eve of its collapse.[1] Like the sultanic Porte at the turn of the 20th century, the Kremlin today seems to be not just relaxing its grip, but losing it.

Gorbachev continues to insist that the adoption of a new all-Union treaty that grants more power to the Union republics can arrest and reverse the centrifugal forces that are pulling the Soviet Union apart and still preserve a federal structure. His constantly reiterated constitutional formula is "strong republics and a strong center," somehow combined in a more perfect and politically "consolidated" Union. However, this formula is merely one of many indications that Gorbachev has become part of the problem (in this case, the nationality problem), not the solution. If Gorbachev had offered the sorts of concessions to national aspirations in 1986 or 1987 that he was willing to offer by 1990, he might have been able to stem the tide. As it is, however, his promises of greater communal autonomy within a still central-ized system fall far short of what nearly all of the formerly "captive nations" of the USSR are demanding and many have in fact already achieved. If any viable solution except dissolution can be found, it will almost certainly have to involve a qualitative reconfiguration of center-periphery relations, not just a quan-titative shift in the existing balance of power. By trying to hold the line, Gorbachev is only prolonging and aggravating what seems to have become, insofar as the survival of the Soviet Union is concerned, a terminal ethnopolitical crisis.

From this perspective, the principal uncertainty facing the U.S. policy community is obviously no longer whether the Soviet Union will evolve into a normal country. It is what the effect on U.S. interests will be as the newly self-assertive peoples of the USSR and the central authorities from whom they are in the process of emancipating themselves continue to work (and fight) out what have already become completely new relationships both with each other and with the outside world. To reduce this uncertainty, U.S. policymakers and policy planners have begun to ask themselves (and their analytical support staffs) a host of novel questions. For purposes of illustration, it suffices to cite the following, security-oriented, examples:

- How confident can we be that the Kremlin will continue to be able to deliver on its international commitments? At a time when the government of Russia is challenging the Kremlin's right to dispose of "Russian" diamonds, gold, and oil without Russia's consent, how farfetched is it to envision a challenge to the Kremlin's agreement to dismantle "Russian" missiles, to suspend the sale of "Russian" arms, or to permit the verification of what is being produced in "Russian" factories?

- How certain is it that the Kremlin will be able to maintain exclusive control of Soviet nuclear weapons and other weapons of mass destruction? At a time when Soviet arsenals are hemorrhaging conventional weapons, what credible guarantees against leakage from putatively more secure facilities are possible? How certain are we that the Soviet high command would be able to distinguish a launch of nuclear weapons by nationalist forces inside the Soviet Union from a foreign attack? Are there any circumstances under which the high command might want to blur the difference?

- How would the implementation of republic sovereignty affect Soviet military capabilities? How much is the Russian government likely to spend on the Soviet armed forces of its own volition? How likely is it to agree to the employment of "its" conscripts outside "its" borders? What happens militarily if the Ukraine acts on its expressed intention to become a nuclear-free zone?

- How would various Soviet republics' achievement of independence—or even sovereignty, which, as they define it, would give their laws precedence over those of the center— affect the correlation of forces in and stability of the various regions and international subsystems of which they would become a part? How would the emergence of independent or quasi-independent Central Asian republics or of an independent or quasi-independent "West Turkestan" affect the security situation in southwestern and northeastern Asia? How would the emergence of an independent Azerbaijan (or northern Azerbaijan) affect the security situation in and around the Persian Gulf? How serious is the threat of a Balkanization of the entire Eurasian continent?

PROTECTING U.S. INTERESTS

The fact that questions such as these are now being raised in Washington, and raised with increasing urgency, is a clear indication of the policy community's recognition that current and emergent developments on the Soviet nationality front could have momentous implications for U.S. interests. To date, however, Washington has made almost no effort to influence the way in which those developments unfold. Although actions we have taken on other "fronts" have affected what is happening on the nationality front, nearly all the effects have been collateral and unintended. Except where Soviet Jewry is concerned, in fact, Washington seems to have gone out of its way to keep ethnopolitical issues off its Soviet affairs agenda.

The greatest inhibition against changing this hands-off policy is Washington's fear that a more activist stance would make it harder to elicit the Kremlin's continued cooperation in liquidating the remnants of the Cold War and in managing the transition to a new world order. At a time when delicate negotiations are under way on such issues as the withdrawal of Soviet troops from Germany and Eastern Europe, the reduction of strategic arms, and Soviet participation in resolving the Persian Gulf crisis, this is certainly a justifiable concern. All things considered, however, it seems far too alarmist with respect to the Kremlin's likely reactions to U.S. diplomatic incursions on the nationality front and far too sanguine about the risks of continued noninterference.

The first point to consider in this connection is that the Kremlin itself has already evinced a willingness to discuss some of the most sensitive aspects of its nationality problem, including the ethnopolitical threat to its exclusive control of Soviet nuclear arms. In addition, it has indicated that it is prepared to permit direct contacts between foreign governments and the governments of the Soviet Union's constituent republics. Quite apart from what the Kremlin has already agreed to, moreover, it very likely would put up with a good deal more before doing anything that might jeopardize its chances of acquiring desperately needed Western economic assistance.

This is not to deny that the Kremlin might feel compelled to retaliate against certain provocations on the nationality front in ways that could threaten U.S. interests. Overreaching by the United States could certainly lead the Kremlin to be somewhat less responsive to U.S. security concerns and perhaps even to slow its by-now irreversible retreat from its residual positions of strength in foreign countries. The Kremlin is already under intense pressure from hawks who are vigorously lobbying for a less dovish Soviet foreign policy. If these hawks could make a convincing case for the proposition (which they have already advanced) that the United States is bound and determined to dismantle not only the Kremlin's external empire, but its internal empire—encompassing what are now Soviet republics—as well, they might become even more influential. Nevertheless, it is hard to envision anything the United States might do that would make such a case seem credible to nonbelievers.

No one in the U.S. policy community today would even consider denouncing the Kremlin as the center of an "evil empire." Nor would Washington adopt a policy of linkage that makes the Kremlin's access to U.S. markets (including credit markets) contingent on its agreement to wholesale decolonization. Absent such ammunition, however, Soviet hawks are unlikely to persuade anyone that the United States is trying to make the nationality front the latest battleground in a continuing Cold War. In consequence, it is hard to see why we should allow the threat posed by the existence of the hawks to continue to justify our observance of a self-imposed, self-denying ordinance against actions on behalf of the ethnopolitical outcomes that would serve our interests. Given the extreme volatility of the nationality front and the multitude of competing claims on scarce American resources, there are obviously strict limits on what we can hope to achieve. At the very least, however, it seems sensible to take a number of relatively low-cost, risk-free steps that might appreciably reduce the likelihood of what would undeniably be highly adverse outcomes, including some outcomes that the Kremlin is as eager as everyone else to avoid.

Some of these steps—and the outcomes they could help to avert—are discussed below.

Nuclear Proliferation. One outcome that we clearly are extremely eager to avert is the fragmentation of control over the Soviet nuclear arsenal and, more particularly, over strategic warheads and missiles. According to press reports, Washington has queried the Kremlin about the reliability of its nuclear security arrangements and received what are described as satisfactory assurances that all is well. Given the growing ideological and ethnopolitical tensions within the Soviet armed forces and the KGB, as well as in the broader society, however, it is difficult to take any such assurances very seriously. Moreover, even if no clear and present danger of a security breakdown exists today, tomorrow could well be another story. In fact, there are a number of far from incredible scenarios under which existing safeguards might fail, including some in which nuclear arms might end up in the hands of groups or governments (including foreign as well as Soviet groups or governments) that are quite hostile to the United States.

To reduce this risk, the U.S. government has every right and reason to demand much firmer assurances than it has received to date that the Kremlin is doing everything possible to prevent the capture, or "liberation," of potentially usable (or recyclable) nuclear weapons. Among other channels, we should use our burgeoning high-level military exchanges with the USSR for this purpose. U.S. participants in these exchanges should voice our concerns urgently and with absolute candor. In the process, they should leave their Soviet interlocutors with no doubt that failure to address and alleviate these concerns will have a seriously adverse effect on U.S.–Soviet relations. At the same time, they should make it clear that *we* are willing to consider making certain changes in *our* strategic posture to minimize the risks that the Soviet high command would undoubtedly perceive in a confidence-building process that might require the unilateral disarmament, dismantling, or relocation of a considerable number of Soviet nuclear weapons. The complex negotiations that would have to ensue could conceivably be folded into accelerated Strategic Arms Reduction Talks II. However, one could also make a strong case for conducting such negotiations as a resumption of the less highly publicized risk reduction talks that led to the creation of the so-called Risk Reduction Center, which is specifically charged with handling a variety of safeguard issues and is an institution whose mandate we should anyway try to broaden in the light of present circumstances.

Russian Fascism. Another horrific outcome of the struggles being waged on the nationality front would be the emergence of a jingoist, neofascist Russia (or rump, Russian-led, Soviet Union). At a minimum, this would mean that men whose values and aspirations are deeply antithetical to our own controlled a large and strategically located part of the earth's surface and a huge, nuclear-armed military force. Furthermore, the probability is very high that the empowerment of these men would be the prelude to an aggressive *anschluss* campaign to protect or restore the rights of the Russian residents or former residents of non-Russian territories. This campaign, in turn, would almost certainly precipitate a bloody internal war—a war that could easily spill across Soviet (or ex-Soviet) borders and have highly destabilizing effects in Eastern Europe, southwestern Asia, and possibly other regions. In consequence, the United States has a very strong interest in enhancing the prestige and ensuring the success of the liberal and democratic leaders who at least for the moment have clearly won the confidence of a large part of the Russian people.

Belated recognition of this interest is presumably at least partially responsible for the recent cessation of derogatory comments about Boris Yeltsin by administration insiders, as well as for the generally more respectful treatment that leading Russian democrats have recently begun to receive from formerly standoffish U.S. officials. Given the growing militancy of right-wing efforts to discredit Russia's democratic officeholders and to sabotage their policies, however, this is clearly too little, especially at a time when Gorbachev seems more disinclined than ever to forge an alliance with the democrats and may well be considering a crackdown against them. What is called for is a much stronger indication by Washington that it cares deeply about the outcome of the struggle that is under way and is prepared to curtail U.S. aid and assistance to the Kremlin if any effort is made to dislodge democratically elected officials.

Looking further down the pike, it would also serve our interests if a sizable portion of the technical assistance we are sending to the Soviet Union was clearly earmarked for programs sponsored or approved by the governments of Moscow, Leningrad, Sverdlovsk, and other democratically led Russian cities, or by the Presidium of the Supreme Soviet of the Russian Soviet Federated Socialist Republic. This would send a clear signal that we are ready to put our money where our mouth is (or should be). It would also make it easier for the democratic recipients to deliver something tangible to their understandably impatient constituents, with all the demonstration effects this would produce.

Islamic Fundamentalism. Still another highly undesirable outcome from a U.S. point of view would be an upsurge of Islamic fundamentalism among the Soviet (or ex-Soviet) Muslims of Central Asia and Azerbaijan. Since much of the information we have on the alleged growth of Islamic fundamentalism in the contemporary USSR comes from Soviet publicists with a clear interest in persuading us to condone the Kremlin's repeated use of military force against Kazakh, Azerbaijani, Uzbek, and other Muslim protesters, estimating the likelihood of such an outcome is difficult. However, information from more trustworthy sources, including intuitively credible information about the lessons many Soviet Muslims have drawn from the ability of fundamentalist forces to drive seemingly omnipotent infidels successively out of Iran and Afghanistan, suggests real cause for concern. Furthermore, all signs indicate that the already fairly widespread proselytizing of the faithful by fundamentalist true believers will become even more extensive with the further erosion of central controls. It is by no means impossible, therefore, that the Muslims of the USSR could be natural allies of some of America's most stubbornly aggressive adversaries (e.g., Iran and Libya) as they reemerge as independent or quasi-independent actors on the international scene.

On its own, the United States can do very little, if anything, to avert this prospect. On the contrary, U.S. efforts to prevent the spread of fundamentalism would almost certainly backfire if, as is likely, they were perceived as such. However, the United States is not impotent. It is in a position to encourage and support such efforts on the part of several antifundamentalist Muslim countries, particularly Turkey. With the exception of 2 million Tajiks, almost all of the Muslims of the USSR are of Turkic origin, speak Turkic languages, and have had positive historical associations with Turks and with Turkey. Hence, in all likelihood, they would be highly receptive to Turkish proposals to open consulates, information centers, trade offices, and other such installations in their midst, and to expand academic, cultural, scientific, and technical exchanges.[2] Thanks to such outreach, the government of Turkey would be in a very good position to provide Soviet Muslims with the most convincing available proof that a Muslim country can become part of the West and successfully modernize itself without undermining its Muslim identity. By vigorously encouraging and generously supporting such outreach, in turn, the U.S. government could help ensure that Islamic fundamentalists do not win over Soviet Muslims largely by default.

Balkanization. A fourth—and, for present purposes, final—outcome that could pose a significant threat to U.S. interests would be the fragmentation of the USSR into a number of highly ethnocentric successor states in which "resident aliens" experience systematic persecution, and the "redress of national grievances" and "rectification of national boundaries" constitute the highest political priorities. The bloody pogroms and border clashes that have already taken place in the Caucasus and Central Asia clearly indicate the kinds of explosive instability such Balkanization could create. It is also indicative—and perhaps even more disturbing in terms of U.S. interests—that the prospect of independence has led the governments or national liberation fronts of the Western borderlands to reassert a variety of long-standing territorial claims not only against Russia but against each other and, in some cases, against their East European neighbors. Given the intensity of the passions invested in many of these disputes, big-time trouble could lie ahead once the disputing parties acquire their own armed forces. This process is already under way in some republics and will most certainly continue and accelerate even in the case of those republics that opt for sovereignty rather than independence (assuming Russia provides such an option by agreeing to link its sovereignty with theirs).

The United States can take a number of steps in the near term to reduce the danger of escalating conflict among the Soviet Union's non-Russian successor states, and between and among them and their neighbors. These include the following:

- Putting the Kremlin on notice that a continuation of its efforts to exacerbate interethnic hostilities could adversely affect U.S.–Soviet relations. These efforts are hard to document conclusively, but a good deal of evidence suggests that the KGB has had a hand in a number of outbreaks of communal violence in the Caucasus and Central Asia, as well as in the emergence of the so-called interfront movements in the Baltic states and several other xenophobically nationalist organizations throughout the USSR. In addition, in a number of instances, the KGB appears to have gone out of its way to try to torpedo efforts by communal leaders to talk out their differences and build bridges between their respective constituencies before national antagonisms got out of hand. Absent a smoking gun, the United States should talk softly on this subject, but it should not hesitate to speak in a way that conveys our strong opposition to the continued use of divide-and-rule tactics at a time when we want conciliation to be high on everyone's agenda.

- Establishing an official U.S. presence in all of the non-

Russian republics and making an all-out effort to contact all important segments of the local populations. Our knowledge of what is actually happening on the ground in most of the non-Russian republics is extremely limited. As a result, we are often at a loss about what to expect next or what, if anything, we might usefully do about it. The prompt opening of miniconsulates of the sort that Washington is considering would be a useful first step, but the United States should take additional steps as quickly as possible, preferably through arrangements made directly with republican rather than central authorities.

- Encouraging and supporting the efforts of communal leaders to open channels of communication with each other and doing everything possible to facilitate bridge-building contacts and exchanges across communal lines. In addition to on-site contacts and exchanges, Washington can organize or help organize roundtable discussions, seminars, and the like on neutral ground, including some in which American participants and other outsiders may be able to play useful roles as mediators and peacemakers in exploring particularly contentious issues.

- Sponsoring and supporting studies to identify and explore the feasibility of cross-border projects that promise to bring significant benefit to all of the participants. Once these studies are completed, the United States should offer to provide or solicit technical and other assistance for cooperative efforts to implement projects that seem likely to have a particularly high yield in terms of interethnic peacekeeping.

- Clearly conveying to everyone concerned that, all other things being equal, U.S. technical assistance and economic aid is more likely to be forthcoming for cross-border projects than for others.

- Making all relevant parties aware that the United States will not provide technical assistance and economic aid to communities that fail to respect the human and communal rights of national minorities within their jurisdictions.

SHORT-TERM FOCUS: PREPARING TO MEET THE CHALLENGE

Needless to say, there is absolutely no guarantee that these and similar steps the United States can prudently take to prevent the centrifugal forces that are tearing the USSR apart from producing worst-case outcomes will actually achieve their intended purpose. In fact, it would not be at all surprising if developments followed Murphy's law and went completely sour, despite our best efforts. This seems particularly likely, since almost all of those efforts involve lead times that are likely to be very long when measured against the accelerating timetable of events. What this suggests, in turn, is that we may eventually have to consider much more drastic, emergency measures to deal with the consequences of our inability to secure more favorable outcomes in the time available. Therefore, it seems none too early to begin at least a certain amount of planning against very undesirable contingencies.

An essay such as this is obviously not an appropriate place to undertake this mind-boggling task. To indicate where the process might end, however, it may not be inappropriate to point out that, among others, we should probably be planning for situations in which the United States cannot effectively protect its interests without deploying, and possibly even employing, military force, either unilaterally or as part of a larger United Nations or multilateral force. Possible cases in point include the acquisition or threatened acquisition of Soviet nuclear weapons by hostile and adventurist groups or regimes, the outbreak or threatened outbreak of large-scale hostilities along or across internationally sensitive Soviet (or ex-Soviet) borders, the initiation of genocidal or potentially genocidal attacks on U.S.-linked ethnic groups (e.g., Jews or Armenians), and/or the outbreak of a Russian civil war pitting an embattled democratic regime against insurgent neofascists. Although the force requirements to deal with these situations would vary greatly, depending on the particularities of the scenario, the need to consider U.S. force requirements in thinking seriously about prospective developments on the Soviet nationality front speaks eloquently for itself.

Given such intimidating prospects, it is not surprising that some of those who have begun to contemplate them have also begun to evince a certain nostalgia for the status quo ante of the early Gorbachev years or even before. In a few cases, in fact, nostalgia has taken hyperbolic form. The British historian E. J. Hobsbawm, for example, has written "in melancholy retrospect" that Brezhnev and his predecessors should be credited with "the great achievement" of saving the citizens of their multinational empire from "the disastrous effects of nationalism." This, however, is clearly giving credit to those who are most to blame for creating and fueling what eventually became an explosion waiting to happen.

This explosion may or may not be about to occur. Even if it cannot be defused, however, it will not vindicate Hobsbawm's argument that the emancipation of the "captive nations" of the USSR is incompatible with the civilized "restructuring of the world in the 21st century."[3] All it will prove is that the consequences of decades of captivity cannot be undone in short order. One of the biggest challenges facing U.S. policymakers today is to do everything they can to undo these consequences. As they try to meet this challenge, misplaced nostalgia, not to mention fatalistic melancholia, can only get in the way.

NOTES

The views expressed are those of the author alone, and do not reflect the views of RAND or any of its clients.

1. See Michael Mandelbaum, "Shaky Empires, Then and Now," *Time*, October 29, 1990, p. 93; see also the writings of Professor Charles Fairbanks at the Johns Hopkins Foreign Policy Institute.
2. See Graham Fuller, "The Emergence of Central Asia," *Foreign Policy*, 78 (Spring 1990), esp. p. 63.
3. See Eric J. Hobsbawm, *Nations and Nationalism Since 1780: Programme, Myth, Reality* (New York: Cambridge University Press, 1990).

APPENDIX I: NATIONALITIES IN THE POPULATION OF THE USSR

TABLE 1. ETHNIC COMPOSITION OF THE FIFTEEN SOVIET REPUBLICS
(Percent)

Republic	Nationality	%	Republic	Nationality	%
Armenia	Armenian	89.7	Latvia	Latvian	53.7
	Azerbaijani	5.5		Russian	32.8
	Russian	2.3		Belorussian	4.5
	Kurd	1.7		Ukrainian	2.7
Azerbaijan	Azerbaijani	78.1		Polish	2.5
	Russian	7.9	Lithuania	Lithuanian	80.1
	Armenian	7.9		Russian	8.6
Belorussia	Belorussian	79.4		Polish	7.7
	Russian	11.9		Belorussian	1.5
	Polish	4.2			
	Ukrainian	2.4	Moldova	Moldovan	63.9
	Jewish	1.4		Ukrainian	14.2
Estonia	Estonian	64.7		Russian	12.8
	Russian	27.9		Gagauzi	3.5
	Ukrainian	2.5		Jewish	2.0
	Belorussian	1.6		Bulgarian	2.0
	Finnish	1.2	Russia	Russian	82.6
Georgia	Georgian	68.8		Tatar	3.6
	Armenian	9.0		Ukrainian	2.7
	Russian	7.4		Chuvash	1.2
	Azerbaijani	5.1		Plus more	
	Osetin	3.3		than 100 other	
	Abkhazian	1.7		nationalities	
Kazakhstan	Russian	40.8	Tajikistan	Tajik	58.8
	Kazakh	36.0		Uzbek	22.9
	Ukrainian	6.1		Russian	10.4
	Tatar	2.1		Tatar	2.1
Kirghizia	Kirghiz	40.7			
	Russian	22.0	Turkmenistan	Turkmen	68.4
	Uzbek	10.3		Russian	12.6
	Ukrainian	2.6		Uzbek	8.5
	Tatar	1.7		Kazakh	2.9

TABLE 1. CONTINUED

Republic	Nationality	%	Republic	Nationality	%
Ukraine	Ukrainian	73.6	Uzbekistan	Uzbek	68.7
	Russian	21.1		Russian	10.8
	Jewish	1.3		Tatar	4.2
	Belorussian	0.8		Kazakh	4.0
	Moldovan	0.6		Tajik	3.9
	Polish	0.5		Karakalpak	1.9

Source: Financial Times, March 12, 1990.

TABLE 2. NUMBERS OF SOVIET CENTRAL ASIANS LIVING IN THE USSR AND ABROAD, 1980 AND 1989

Nationality	USSR (1989)	Abroad (1980)
Karakalpak	423,000	2,000 (Afghanistan)
Kazakh	8,138,000	800,000 (China)
		3,000 (Afghanistan)
Kirghiz	2,531,000	97,000 (China)
		25,000 (Afghanistan)
Tajik	4,217,000	
Turkmen	2,718,000	300,000 (Afghanistan)
		400,000 (Iran)
Uigur	262,000	5,000,000 (China)
Uzbek	16,686,000	18,000 (China)
		1,500,000 (Afghanistan)

Source: Compiled by Ronald Grigor Suny from the following: Ann Sheehy, "Ethnic Muslims Account for Half of the Soviet Population Increase," *Report on the USSR* 2, no. 3 (January 19, 1990), pp. 16–18; and Azade-Ayse Rorlich, "Soviet Central Asians Look Towards Xinjiang," *Report on the USSR* 1, no. 50 (December 15, 1989), pp. 21–23.

SOVIET POPULATION TRENDS, 1979–1989[1]

□ Russians represented 50.8 percent of the Soviet population in 1989, down from 52.4 percent in 1979.

□ Slavs represented 69.74 percent of the Soviet population in 1989, down from 72.19 percent in 1979 and 73.97 percent in 1970.

□ Russians have been migrating out of the southern Soviet republics and have declined absolutely in number in Armenia, Azerbaijan, Georgia, Tajikistan, Turkmenistan, and Uzbekistan. This trend began in the 1960s in Transcaucasia and in the 1970s in Central Asia; the opposite trend is apparent in Latvia, where Slavic in-migration in the 1980s exceeded the increase of the indigenous populations. The proportion of Russians has also increased significantly in Belorussia, Lithuania, Moldova, and the Ukraine.

□ The Muslim and Caucasian peoples, as well as the Moldovans, have increased their share of the overall Soviet population. Central Asian Muslims plus Azerbaijanis make up 14.39 percent of the Soviet population; Armenians and Georgians together, 4 percent; Moldovans 1.17 percent; and Baltic peoples only 1.94 percent.

□ Traditionally Muslim peoples, who now number 54.8 million (excluding Osetins, Abkhazians, Ajars, and a few other small groups), make up 19.2 percent of the Soviet population. As Table 3 indicates, they had the largest proportional population increase, while Baltic and Slavic peoples had the lowest (below the average increase for the Soviet population as a whole).

□ The population of Turkic-speaking peoples, the second largest linguistic group after the Slavs, numbers 49.5 million (17.3 percent of the Soviet population) and increased somewhat slower than the Muslim population in general (at a rate of 24.5 percent). The five Turkic Muslim peoples that have republics of their own decreased their rate of population growth in the 1980s, though it still remains high.

TABLE 3. PERCENTAGE POPULATION INCREASE OF VARIOUS
NATIONALITIES IN THE USSR, 1979–1989

Nationality	Population increase (%)
Tajik	45.5
Uzbek	34.0
Turkmen	34.0
Kirghiz	32.8
Kazakh	24.1
Azerbaijani	24.0
Moldovan	13.0
Georgian	11.6
Armenian	11.5
Soviet population as a whole	9.0
Lithuanian	7.6
Belorussian	6.0
Russian	5.6
Ukrainian	4.2
Latvian	1.4
Estonian	0.7

Source: Ann Sheehy, "Russian Share of Soviet Population Down to 50.8 Percent," *Report on the USSR* 1, no. 42 (October 20, 1989), p. 2.

□ The Soviet population as a whole grew at a slower annual rate in the 1980s than it did in the 1970s; for the Tajiks, Moldovans, Belorussians, and Latvians, growth was faster in the 1980s. The sharp drop in the Armenian growth rate is probably due to the losses suffered in the earthquake of December 7, 1988, and emigration to the United States.

□ Nationalities that do not have their own republic and that declined in number in the 1970s continued to decline in the 1980s (Mordvins, Karelians, and Finns); the Jewish population also declined (by 20 percent), though here emigration was a principal factor. Some small nationalities—Meskhetians, Crimean Tatars, Krymchaks (Crimean Jews)—reappeared in the latest census, while others—like the Veps—reversed their declines.

□ Use of one's native language remains high overall. It is

increasing among Armenians and Estonians; decreasing slightly among Belorussians, Ukrainians, and Moldovans; and holding fairly steady among the rest.

NOTE

1. The Soviet population trends are from: Ann Sheehy, "Russian Share of Soviet Population Down to 50.8 Percent," *Report on the USSR* 1, no. 42 (October 20, 1989), pp. 1–5; ———, "Ethnic Muslims Account for Half of the Soviet Population Increase," *Report on the USSR* 2, no. 3 (January 19, 1990), pp. 15–18.

APPENDIX II: SYMPOSIUM ON SOVIET NATIONALITIES AND AMERICAN FOREIGN POLICY

Organized by the Council on Foreign Relations in cooperation with the Nationality and Siberian Studies Program of Columbia University's Harriman Institute

October 25–26, 1990

Michael Mandelbaum, Group Director—*Council on Foreign Relations*
Jeremy R. Azrael, Author—*RAND*
Sergei Maksudov, Author—*Harvard University*
Alexander J. Motyl, Author—*Columbia University*
Ronald Grigor Suny, Author—*University of Michigan*
William Taubman, Author—*Amherst College*
Theresa F. Weber, Rapporteur—*Council on Foreign Relations*
Audrey McInerney, Rapporteur—*Council on Foreign Relations*

Ivo Banac—*Yale University*
Aurel Braun—*University of Toronto*
Robert Cullen—Soviet-American Trade
James Davis—*Columbia University*
William M. Drennan—*Colonel, U.S. Air Force, Visiting Military Fellow, Council on Foreign Relations*
Eric Edelman—*U.S. Department of Defense*
Felice Gaer—*International League for Human Rights*
Mark Garrison—*Brown University*
Wallace C. Gregson—*Colonel, U.S. Marine Corps, Visiting Military Fellow, Council on Foreign Relations*
Michael Haltzel—*Woodrow Wilson International Center for Scholars*
Peter Hauslohner—*U.S. Department of State*

Grey Hodnett—*U.S. Central Intelligence Agency*
Henry Huttenbach—*City College of New York*
Edward Kline—*Czekhov Publishing Corporation*
James Klurfeld—Newsday
Ivo Lederer—*SRI International*
William Luers—*Metropolitan Museum of Art*
Margaret Osmer-McQuade—*Council on Foreign Relations*
Jenik Radon—*Radon and Ishizumi*
Jaan Rebane—*Institute of Philosophy, Sociology and Law, Tallin, Estonia*
Cynthia Roberts—*Hunter College*
Michael Rywkin—*City College of New York*
Sophia Sluzar—Problems of Communism
Alexander Vershbow—*U.S. Department of State*

INDEX

Abkhazians, 12, 79
Alexander III, Tsar, 25
All-Union treaty, 59, 90
Angola, 51
Armenia, 9; diaspora populations, 79; ethnic conflicts, 2, 64, 78–79; independence movement following civil war, 29–30; intelligentsia's loss of influence, 78; militias, 76; 1917 nationalist movement, 38; political efforts of nationalists, 74; purges of top leaders, 74; Turkey and, 82–83
Arms control, 1, 57, 60–61, 94–95
Astrakhan, 20
Autocracy, Tsarist empire and, 20–22
Azerbaijan: diaspora populations, 79, 81–83; ethnic conflicts, 2, 64, 78–79; independence movement following civil war, 29–30; intelligentsia's loss of influence, 78; Iranian Azerbaijanis and, 81–82; militias, 76; 1917 nationalist movement, 38; political efforts of nationalists, 74

Baku, 68
Balkanization of Soviet areas, possible, 97–98
Baltic republics. *See* Estonia; Latvia; Lithuania
Basmachis, 28, 30
Belorussia, 32, 49–50; Western states' interest in, 54–58
Bessarabia, 32
Bolshevik policy on nationalities, 72
Borders, sanctity of, 11
Brezhnev, Leonid I., 35, 36, 69
Budenny, Gen. Semyon, 30

Bukhara, 30
Bukovina, 32
Bulgaria, 48, 53

Catherine II, the Great, 4, 21, 26
Chanturia, Giorgi, 78
China, People's Republic of, 48
Civil war in 1990s, possible, 12–13, 50
Clausewitz, Karl von, 1
Coexistence, 36–37
Collectivization, 31, 69
Confederation of post-Soviet states, 59, 84
Cossacks, 21
Crimean Tatars, 2, 21, 32, 35
Crimean War, 23
Custine, Marquis de, 22
Czechoslovakia, 32, 35, 36, 48, 53–54, 56

Decolonization process, 6–7
Decommunization, 53, 61
Demirchian, Karen, 74
Detotalization process, 44–45; chaos resulting from miscalculations, 46–48; Eastern Europe and, 48–49; economic problems and, 45–46; glasnost and, 45, 46; independence for republics and, 49–51; political reforms and, 46, 47. *See also* State-building following detotalization
Diaspora populations, 7–8, 79–80; Azerbaijan-Iran situation, 81–82; in United States, 85
Dictatorship, Soviet empire and, 30–31, 33
Diplomatic relations between republics and West, proposed, 59

111

ABOUT THE AUTHORS

Jeremy R. Azrael is a senior member of the International Policy Department of RAND. Before joining RAND, he served as a member of the Secretary's Policy Planning Council at the Department of State. Between 1961 and 1981, Azrael was on the faculty of the University of Chicago, where he was Professor of Political Science and Chairman of the Committee on Slavic Area Studies. He is the author of numerous articles and books on Soviet affairs, including *The KGB in Kremlin Politics* (1989), *Soviet Nationality Policies and Practices* (1978), and *East-West Relations: Controlling A Long-Term Conflict* (1977).

Sergei Maksudov (Alexander Babyonyshev) is a Fellow at the Harvard Russian Research Center and teaches in the Slavic Department at Harvard University. He has also taught at Boston University and the University of Alberta in Canada. Born in the USSR, he emigrated to the United States in 1981. He is the author of *Losses of Population in the USSR* (1989) and *Unheard Voices: Documents of Smolensk Archive* (1987), and is the editor of *On Sakharov* (1981).

Alexander J. Motyl is Associate Professor of Political Science and Director of the Nationality and Siberian Studies Program of the W. Averell Harriman Institute for Advanced Study of the Soviet Union at Columbia University. He is the author of *Sovietology, Rationality, Nationality: Coming to Grips with Nationalism in the USSR* (1990), *Will the Non-Russians Rebel? State, Ethnicity, and Stability in the USSR* (1987), and numerous articles on Soviet affairs.

Ronald Grigor Suny is Alex Manoogian Professor of Modern Armenian History at the University of Michigan. He is the author of *The Making of the Georgian Nation* (1988), *Armenia in the Twentieth Century* (1983), and *The Baku Commune, 1917–1918: Class and Nationality in the Russian Revolution* (1972), as well as editor of and contributor to a number of books including, *Trans-caucasia, Nationalism and Social Change* (1983). He is currently writing a study of Stalin and the formation of the nationalities issues in the Soviet Union.

William Taubman is Bertrand Snell Professor of Political Science at Amherst College and a Fellow at the Harvard Russian Research Center. He is the author of *Stalin's American Policy* (1982) and *Governing Soviet Cities* (1973), coauthor with Jane A. Taubman of *Moscow Spring* (1989), and editor and translator of Sergei Khrushchev's book, *Khrushchev on Khrushchev* (1990). He is currently working on his own biography of Nikita Khrushchev.

Michael Mandelbaum is Director of the Project on East-West Relations at the Council on Foreign Relations and Christian A. Herter Professor of American Foreign Policy at the Paul H. Nitze School of Advanced International Studies at Johns Hopkins University. He is the author of a number of books including: *The Fate of Nations: The Search for National Security in the 19th and 20th Centuries* (1988); with Seweryn Bialer, *The Global Rivals* (1988); and with Strobe Talbott, *Reagan and Gorbachev* (1987).

The Council on Foreign Relations publishes authoritative and timely books on international affairs and American foreign policy. Designed for the interested citizen and specialist alike, the Council's rich assortment of studies covers topics ranging from economics to regional conflict to East-West relations. If you would like more information, please write:

Council on Foreign Relations Press
58 East 68th Street
New York, NY 10021
Telephone: (212) 734-0400
Fax: (212) 861-1789 or 861-1849